W9-CXP-068

The American Heritage®

Essential Student Thesaurus

Second Edition

Houghton Mifflin Company

Boston • New York

Editorial Staff

Steve Kleinedler
Project Editor

Kristen Patey
Associate Editor

Editorial Staff, First Edition

Laura P. Chesterton   David A. Jost
Ann-Marie Imbornoni   Beth G. Rowen

Production Staff

Christopher Leonesio
Vice President, Managing Editor

Christopher Granniss
Database Production Supervisor

James W. Mitchell
Production and Manufacturing
Supervisor

Joyce Weston
Text Design

Library of Congress Cataloging-in-Publication Data

American Heritage essential student thesaurus
    The American Heritage essential student thesaurus.—2nd ed.
        p. cm
    Includes index.
    Summary: More than 200 alphabetically arranged entries give synonyms, definitions, and parts of speech, with example sentences for each synonym to distinguish shades of meaning.   ISBN 0-618-28017-0
    1. English language—Synonyms and antonyms—Juvenile literature. [1. English language—Synonyms and antonyms.] I. Title: Essential student thesaurus. II. Houghton Mifflin Company. III. Title.
PE1591 .A53 2003
423'.1—dc21   2002038761

Manufactured in the United States of America

Introduction

Why use a thesaurus?

A thesaurus is a book that lists synonyms and antonyms. Synonyms are words that share the same or nearly the same meaning. Antonyms are words that have opposite or nearly opposite meanings.

Understanding how to use synonyms and antonyms is one of the secrets of good writing. Let's imagine you are writing a letter to distant cousins who have never seen snow. You want to describe a really harsh winter, so you begin:

> *Of course, winter is normally a **cold** time of year, but last January was unbelievably **cold**. I would go outside wearing two pairs of socks and boots, and my feet would still feel **cold**! I couldn't wait for spring to arrive so the **cold** weather would end.*

You realize something seems wrong. Your words just don't communicate the idea you want to get across, and your cousins aren't going to think they have been missing much. How can you make the story sound more exciting? You decide to try your new book, *The American Heritage Essential Student Thesaurus,* and see if it can help. You look up the adjective *cold* and read this note:

cold   cold, chilly, frigid, frosty, icy

These adjectives all describe something at a very low temperature. *The **cold** wind made me wish I had worn a coat. They walked to the store even though the autumn day felt **chilly**. Gordon brought the heater into the **frigid** room. This **frosty** weather is perfect for sledding. The travelers warmed their **icy** hands by the fire.*

Antonym: hot

Maybe you can improve your letter after all, simply by changing a few words:

> *Of course, winter is normally a **chilly** time of year, but last January was unbelievably **frigid**. I would go outside wearing two pairs*

*of socks and boots, and my feet would still feel **icy**! I couldn't wait
for spring to arrive so the **cold** weather would end.*

There is nothing wrong with the word *cold*, but if you repeat any word
too many times in the same paragraph your writing will sound flat and boring,
no matter how exciting the story you are telling. Choosing among different
words with similar meanings also helps you express precisely what you want
to say. Suppose you continue your letter this way:

*As soon as the weather warms up, the icicles fall and **break**. You
can hear the ice **break** too as the river starts flowing again.*

You feel that these sentences could be improved as well. First of all, you
would rather not repeat the word *break*. You would rather use language that
better describes the different sights and sounds of breaking icicles and ice. You
look up the verb *break* in *The American Heritage Essential Student Thesaurus*
and read this note:

break   break, crack, split, splinter, shatter

These verbs mean to separate or to cause something to separate
into parts or pieces. ***Break*** is the most general: *Take care not
to **break** anything while you're dusting.* ***Crack*** means to break,
often with a sharp snapping sound, without dividing into parts:
*We heard the ice **cracking** as we walked on it.* ***Split*** means to
divide along something's length: *These pants have **split** along
the seam.* ***Splinter*** means to split into long, thin, sharp pieces:
*Lightning struck the tree and **splintered** it.* ***Shatter*** means to
break into many loose scattered pieces: *The perfume bottle fell
and **shattered** on the floor.*

You realize how easy it is to rewrite the sentences, making them more
accurate, descriptive, and interesting:

*As soon as the weather warms up, the icicles fall and **shatter**.
You can hear the ice **crack** too as the river starts flowing again.*

By now you can see that *The American Heritage Essential Student Thesaurus*
includes two different types of entries. One type of entry lists words that share
a related definition but do not all mean exactly the same thing. A separate

meaning is given for each of the words to explain how they vary from the shared definition. *Break* is an example of this type of entry. Another example is the adjective *dirty*:

dirty   dirty, filthy, foul, grimy

These adjectives apply to what is unclean, impure, or unkempt. ***Dirty***, the most general, describes what is covered or stained with dirt: ***Dirty*** *dishes were piled up in the sink.* ***Filthy*** means disgustingly dirty: *Put that* ***filthy*** *shirt in the washing machine right away.* ***Foul*** suggests gross offensiveness, particularly to the sense of smell: *A layer of algae covered the* ***foul*** *pond.* ***Grimy*** describes something whose surface is smudged with dirt such as grime or soot: *I found this* ***grimy*** *pair of gloves near the gardening tools.*

The other type of entry lists words that can all mean close to the same thing. *Cold* is an example of this type of entry. Another example is the noun *plan*:

plan   plan, design, project, scheme, strategy

These nouns all mean a method or program that is thought out to guide one in doing something. *Tom has no vacation* ***plans*** *yet. The car manufacturers published their* ***designs*** *of next year's models. I have several* ***projects*** *for my spring vacation. We're coming up with a new* ***scheme*** *to save energy. What* ***strategy*** *will you use at this point in the chess game?*

Every word in every entry includes a sample sentence, printed in *italics*, to give you a model of how that word can be used.

If you cann't find the word you are looking for, try the index in the back of this book. The index lists all of the words included in the entries. If you looked up *fury*, for example, you would learn that *fury* is one of the synonyms in the note at the word *anger*.

This newly revised second edition of *The American Heritage Essential Student Thesaurus* has been greatly expanded to provide you with even more word choices. We hope you have fun using it to express yourself with imagination!

ability ability, talent, skill, aptitude

These nouns refer to qualities in a person that allow or help one to succeed at something. ***Ability*** is the mental or physical power to do something: *Nothing seems to interfere with Charlie's* ***ability*** *to concentrate.* ***Talent*** means ability one is born with, especially ability in the arts: *Maureen's* ***talent*** *in drawing is sure to win her a scholarship.* ***Skill*** stresses ability that one gets or develops through experience: *Your* ***skill*** *in writing has improved this term.* ***Aptitude*** means the ability to learn, understand, or perform, especially an ability one is born with: *Emily has a special* ***aptitude*** *for solving extremely complicated math problems.*

accompany accompany, conduct, escort, chaperone

These verbs mean to be with or to go with another person or other people. ***Accompany*** suggests that the people involved are peers or equals: *I went to the gymnasium* ***accompanied*** *by my friends.* ***Conduct*** refers to the guidance of others: *The usher* ***conducted*** *the patrons to their seats in the theater.* ***Escort*** stresses that the guidance offers protection: *The bodyguards* ***escorted*** *the mayor through the crowd.* ***Chaperone*** specifies the supervision by adults of young persons: *The teachers will* ***chaperone*** *students during the field trip to the zoo.*

acknowledge acknowledge, admit, confess

These verbs mean to make known that something is true or a fact, usually with reluctance or under pressure. ***Acknowledge*** means to accept responsibility for something one makes known: *Ellen* ***acknowledged*** *that she had made a mistake.* ***Admit*** usually means to acknowledge one's acts or accept a different point of view with noticeable unwillingness: *I* ***admit*** *there may be better ways to make a decision, but I was in a hurry.* ***Confess*** usually means to admit to something that is harmful or inconvenient to oneself: *We have to* ***confess*** *that we lied about the dent in the car.*

active   active, energetic, dynamic, lively

These adjectives mean engaged in activity. **Active**, the most neutral, means being in a state of action as opposed to being passive: *His grandparents are still **active** and healthy people.* **Energetic** suggests action with tireless enthusiasm and spirit: *Those are the most **energetic** volunteers I've ever seen.* **Dynamic** means having energy and forcefulness that often inspires other people: *A **dynamic** speaker, the senator often persuades her colleagues to change their votes.* **Lively** means alert, animated, and energetic: *We had a **lively** discussion about the presidential election.*

adapt   adapt, accommodate, adjust, conform

These verbs mean to change something to make it suitable. *Human beings can **adapt** themselves to a wide variety of climates. I cannot **accommodate** myself to the new rules. If you **adjust** your seat belt, you will be more comfortable. He wore shorts to school the first day but later **conformed** to the dress code.*

adventurous   adventurous, adventuresome, daredevil, daring

These adjectives mean to be willing to take risks. ***Adventurous** pioneers traveled westward. The **adventuresome** prospector explored the valley for possible sites to mine for gold. The **daredevil** motorcyclist jumped over a row of parked buses. We watched the **daring** acrobats swing from the trapeze without the safety of a net below.*

affect   affect, influence, touch, move

These verbs mean to produce a mental or emotional effect. To **affect** is to act upon a person's emotions: *Negative book reviews didn't **affect** the author's attitude at all.* **Influence** suggests a degree of control or sway over a person's thinking, actions, and emotions: *The article **influenced** his decision to buy a new car this year.* **Touch** usually means to inspire a tender response, such as love, gratitude, or compassion: *I was **touched** by your kind offer to help.* **Move** suggests profound emotional effect that sometimes leads to action or has a further consequence: *The account of the refugee's experiences **moved** us to tears.*

agree

agree, correspond, conform, coincide

These verbs indicate a harmony or compatibility between people or things. ***Agree*** often suggests harmony through acceptance of ideas or actions and thus adaptation: *We finally **agreed** on which day to have the party.* ***Correspond*** refers to similarity, for example, in use, character, form, or design: *The Parliament in Great Britain **corresponds** to the Congress of the United States.* ***Conform*** means to correspond in nature or basic characteristics, sometimes in order to adjust to established standards: *If you would like to keep your borrowing privileges, you must **conform** to the library's rules.* ***Coincide*** means to agree exactly in space, time, or thought: *Kathy and David's opinions **coincide** on the topic of homeschooling.*

Antonym: disagree

aim

aim, direct, level, point, train

These verbs mean to turn something in the direction of a goal or target. *The photographer **aimed** the camera at the wedding guests. Students were advised to **direct** their eyes to their own papers. The reporter **leveled** criticism at the administration. The witness **pointed** a finger at the suspect. Before you shoot, be sure to **train** your gun toward the target.*

alone

alone, solitary, lonesome, lonely

These adjectives describe being apart from others. ***Alone*** means lacking a companion but not necessarily feeling unhappy about it: *I walked **alone** on the beach while my brother went surfing.* ***Solitary*** often means being physically apart from others by choice: *Matt enjoys **solitary** activities such as reading and painting.* ***Lonesome*** means wishing for a companion: *Tommy thought the goldfish looked **lonesome*** *in its glass bowl.* **Lonely** often means sad at being by oneself: *Jill felt* **lonely** *while all her friends were away on vacation.*

amuse

amuse, entertain, regale

These verbs refer to actions that provide pleasure, especially as a means of passing time. **Amuse** suggests directing the attention away from serious matters: *I* **amused** *myself with a game of solitaire.* **Entertain** means to hold the attention in an agreeable way: *Computers can* **entertain** *as well as educate.* To **regale** is to entertain with something that is very enjoyable: *Matt* **regaled** *us with funny stories about his vacation.*

anger

anger, rage, fury, indignation

These nouns refer to different degrees of strong displeasure. **Anger** is the most general: *We could sense his* **anger** *about the mix-up.* **Rage** and **fury** mean strong and often destructive anger: *Their insensitive comments filled me with* **rage**. *In her* **fury** *at being teased, Amy threw Jason's books down the stairs.* **Indignation** is anger at something wrongful, unjust, or evil: *The incident aroused the* **indignation** *of everyone in town.*

annoy

annoy, irritate, bother, provoke

These verbs mean to disturb or trouble a person, causing moderate anger. **Annoy** means to disturb someone mildly by an act that tries his or her patience: *The sound of footsteps on the bare floor* **annoyed** *the downstairs neighbors.* **Irritate** is somewhat stronger in tone: *His constant interruptions* **irritated** *everyone at the meeting.* **Bother** means to cause someone a troublesome inconvenience: *I'm sorry to* **bother** *you by calling so late at night, but I have important news.* **Provoke** means to make someone angry, often on purpose: *The reporter's obnoxious questions would* **provoke** *anyone.*

answer

answer, respond, reply, retort

These verbs refer to different kinds of reactions. **Answer**, **respond**, and **reply** mean to speak, write, or act in response to something: *Please **answer** my question. I didn't expect the President to **respond** personally to my letter. The visiting team scored three runs, and the home team **replied** with two of their own.* **Retort** means to answer verbally in a quick, sharp, or witty way: *"My shoes may not be new, but at least they're clean!" Terry **retorted**.*

Antonym: ask

anxiety

anxiety, worry, care, concern

These nouns refer to troubled states of mind. **Anxiety** suggests feelings of fear and apprehension: *The patient had feelings of **anxiety** and helplessness whenever he faced stressful situations.* **Worry** implies the ongoing presence of doubt or fear: *She **worried** that she would not be able to finish the complex project before the deadline.* **Care** refers to the state of mind of a person who has a great deal of responsibility: *The manager's face was worn with **care**.* **Concern** suggests serious thought along with emotion: *The principal had a great deal of **concern** for the well-being of the students.*

appreciate

appreciate, value, prize, treasure, cherish

These verbs mean to have a favorable opinion of someone or something. **Appreciate** means to judge highly in comparison with something else: *That awful restaurant certainly taught me to **appreciate** home cooking.* **Value** means to have a high opinion of something's importance or worth: *A true democracy **values** the free exchange of ideas.* **Prize** often suggests feeling pride in owning something: *Steve **prizes** the movie star's autograph so highly that he is making a frame for it.* **Treasure** and **cherish** both mean to care for attentively and affectionately: *Susan **treasures** that quilt because it has been in her family for generations. A solid friendship is something to **cherish**.*

apprehend

apprehend, comprehend, understand, grasp

These verbs refer to an awareness of the nature and importance of something. **Apprehend** implies an awareness of something that is realized due to emotions or the senses: *People with a good sense of smell can* **apprehend** *objects by their scent.* **Comprehend** and **understand** both stress complete realization and knowledge: *Do you* **comprehend** *how important it is to wear a seat belt? Since the students* **understood** *the material that was explained in the introduction, the teacher continued on to the first chapter.* To **grasp** is to take an idea and hold onto it tightly: *Once the mayor* **grasped** *the extent of the crisis, she lobbied the state legislature for funding.*

approve   approve, endorse, sanction, certify, ratify

These verbs mean to express a favorable opinion or to show satisfaction or acceptance. **Approve** means to consider something to be right or good: *My teacher does not* **approve** *of talking in class without raising your hand.* **Endorse** implies the expression of support, often by making a statement in public: *The American Dental Association* **endorses** *certain brands of toothpaste.* **Sanction** refers to approval that is authorized by an official: *Voting is a right that is granted to all citizens and* **sanctioned** *by law.* **Certify** implies that official approval is the result of meeting requirements or standards: *In this state, hair salons must be* **certified** *by the Board of Health before they are allowed to serve the public.* To **ratify** something is to make it legally enforceable by official approval: *New amendments to the Constitution must be* **ratified** *by Congress and three-fourths of the state legislatures.*

argue   argue, quarrel, bicker

These verbs mean to exchange words expressing disagreement about positions or opinions. **Argue** means to discuss something with someone who has a different point of view, especially in order to persuade that person to agree with you: *It's rare to find a person who can* **argue** *without getting angry or emotional.* **Quarrel** means to argue in an unfriendly or even hateful way: *I don't want to* **quarrel** *with you over something so unimportant.* **Bicker** refers to sharp, continuous, bad-tempered quarreling: *The children were* **bickering** *about the same thing for days.*

ask

ask, inquire, question, examine, quiz

These verbs mean to seek information. *Ask* and *inquire* are the most general: *Rosa stopped at the gas station and **asked** for directions to the stadium. Chris went into the store to **inquire** about the "Help Wanted" sign in the window.* **Question** often means to ask a series of questions: *The lawyer **questioned** the witness in great detail about the robbery.* **Examine** often means to question in order to test someone's knowledge: *All of their real estate agents have been **examined** and licensed by the state board.* **Quiz** means to question students in an informal test: *The teacher will **quiz** us tomorrow on the multiplication tables.*

Antonym: answer

authentic

authentic, genuine, real, true

These adjectives mean not counterfeit or copied. *An expert assured us that the chair is an **authentic** antique, made in the eighteenth century. The recipe calls for **genuine** Italian olive oil, but the store sells only Greek brands. The bouquets were made with silk flowers instead of **real** ones. A **true** friend would be more understanding.*

average

average, medium, mediocre, fair

These adjectives refer to a rank or position around the middle of some type of scale. *Average* and *medium* describe something midway between extremes, usually something that is enough for the purpose in question but lacks distinction: *In spite of all their extra advertisements, the store did an **average** night's business. Next, chop up an onion of **medium** size.* **Mediocre** stresses the undistinguished aspect of what is average: *The movie was a **mediocre** comedy at best.* **Fair** means passable but substantially below excellent: *Ted is **fair** at sports, but he's a fine musician.*

aware

aware, conscious, alert, vigilant

These adjectives mean paying close attention to or mindful of something. *Aware* refers to knowledge that is obtained by hearing, seeing, feeling, smelling, or touching; by perception, such as the attitudes of other people; or by information: *I became* **aware** *of the smell of gasoline. She became* **aware** *of her grandmother's presence in the room. Aren't you* **aware** *that there's a law against littering?* **Conscious** stresses the recognition of something that is sensed or felt: *Most of his friends weren't* **conscious** *of the fact that English was not his first language.* **Alert** stresses the quickness to recognize something and respond to it: *The soldiers remained* **alert** *to enemy gunfire.* **Vigilant** means to be on the look out for something that is or might be dangerous: *The inspector kept a* **vigilant** *eye on every building where a fire could start.*

bad

bad, evil, wicked

These adjectives describe something associated with wrong. **Bad**, the most general, describes something unpleasant, offensive, incorrect, or responsible for wrongdoing: *What with the snowstorms and all the ice, we really have had* **bad** *weather all month.* **Evil** means bad in a way that causes harm and suggests an influence that makes others bad too: *The dictator had an* **evil** *plan to take over the world.* **Wicked** suggests doing wrong on purpose: *You are* **wicked** *to play such a cruel trick on the neighbors.*

Antonym: good

banish

banish, exile, deport, transport, extradite

These verbs mean to send away from a country or state. **Banish** applies to the forced departure from a country as the result of an official order: *The traitor was* **banished** *from the kingdom.* **Exile** refers to the leaving of one's country, either willingly in order to avoid unfavorable conditions or unwillingly by being legally forced to go. *When the government was overthrown, the royal family was* **exiled**. **Deport** means to force a foreigner to leave the country: *The judge* **deported** *the workers who had entered the country illegally.* **Transport** refers to sending a person abroad, especially sending a criminal to a penal colony: *Centuries ago, British criminals were **transported** to Australia.* **Extradite** applies to delivering a person who has been accused or convicted of a crime to the state or country that has legal authority over him or her: *The court refused to **extradite** political refugees.*

beautiful

beautiful, lovely, pretty

These adjectives describe something that gives pleasure or enjoyment by appealing to one's tastes. **Beautiful** means pleasing to the senses, to the mind, or both: *What's the name of that **beautiful** song you're playing?* **Lovely** means attractive in a way that appeals to one's emotions: *The singer won over the audience at once with her **lovely** voice.* **Pretty** means beautiful in a delicate or graceful way: *My aunt wrote to me on some of her **prettiest** scented stationery.*

Antonym: ugly

begin

begin, commence, start, embark

These verbs mean to take the first step or to get working or moving. **Begin** is the most general word: *The movie **begins** at eight o'clock.* **Commence** is a more formal word than begin: *Our meetings always **commence** with a call to order.* **Start** often means to begin from a standstill: *The train **started** as soon as Jason sat down.* **Embark** means to set out on a venture or journey: *After graduating from college in June, Maria will **embark** on a cross-country trip.*

Antonym: end

bend

bend, curve, round

These verbs mean to swerve or cause to swerve from a straight line. **Bend** *your knees when you lift something off the ground. This road **curves** sharply up ahead. The line at the ticket window was so long that it **rounded** the corner.*

Antonym: straighten

beneficial   beneficial, profitable, advantageous

These adjectives apply to what promotes a result or gain that is favorable or positive. ***Beneficial*** is used to describe something that enhances health, happiness, or prosperity: *Anne found that a temperate climate was **beneficial** to her health.* ***Profitable*** refers to what results in material gain or useful compensation: *Ashley's speculation on the stock market was very **profitable**; she made half a million dollars.* Something ***advantageous*** provides improvement in position or in chances of success: *The treasurer signed a contract that is **advantageous** to our company.*

besides   besides, too, also, likewise, furthermore

These adverbs mean in addition to something else. ***Besides*** often introduces something that reinforces what has gone before it: *We don't feel like cooking; **besides**, there is no food in the house.* ***Too*** is the most casual, used in everyday speech: *If you're going to the library today, I'd like to go **too**.* ***Also*** is more formal: *Brian is usually very friendly, but he is **also** capable of bearing a grudge.* ***Likewise*** is even more formal: *Their parents were planning on attending the ceremony and **likewise** the reception to follow.* ***Furthermore*** often stresses that the clause following it is more important than the preceding clause: *I don't want you to go to that place; **furthermore**, I forbid it.*

boast   boast, brag, crow

These verbs mean to speak with pride, often too much pride, about oneself or something related to oneself, such as one's possessions. ***Boast*** is the most general: *I can't stand hearing them constantly **boast** about all the fancy places they have visited.* ***Brag*** suggests making exaggerated claims or showing a conceited attitude: *He **bragged** that he could run faster than anyone in the world.* ***Crow*** means to boast with loud rejoicing, as over a victory: *Don't **crow** over the score before the game is over!*

boring　boring, dull, tedious, tiresome

These adjectives mean lacking in interest, liveliness, or imagination. *Boring* describes something that makes one feel tired and unhappy: *The movie was so **boring** that half the audience fell asleep.* *Dull* means uninteresting and unsurprising: *The lecturer somehow managed to give a great presentation on a **dull** topic.* *Tedious* describes something that is boring because of its slowness: *Wendy thinks train travel is romantic, but we find it **tedious**.* *Tiresome* means tedious and repetitious: *It's a **tiresome** job returning bottles and cans, but I like helping the environment.*

Antonyms: interesting, lively

brave　brave, courageous, fearless, bold, valiant

These adjectives mean having or showing courage in a difficult or dangerous situation. *Brave*, the most general, often refers to an inner quality: *I'm not **brave** enough to speak in front of such a large crowd.* *Courageous* means consciously drawing on one's inner strength to face peril: *The **courageous** captain guided the ship through the terrible storm.* *Fearless* emphasizes the absence of fear: *The **fearless** tightrope walker does not use a net.* *Bold* often means being brave and showing a tendency to seek out danger: *The **bolder** members of the search party went into the cave first.* *Valiant* means brave in a heroic way. It is usually used when describing a person: *The **valiant** firefighters had rescued everyone from the burning building.*

Antonym: cowardly

breach　breach, infraction, violation, transgression, infringement

These nouns mean an act or instance of breaking a law or regulation or failing to fulfill a duty, obligation, or promise. *Breach* and *infraction* are the least specific: *Revealing a secret would be a **breach** of trust. In most sports, **infractions** of the rules will result in a penalty.* A *violation* is committed knowingly and with complete lack of regard for legal, moral, or ethical considerations: *Failure to show up for spring training was a **violation** of the baseball player's contract.* **Transgression** often applies to divine or moral law: *During confession, I told the priest I was sorry for my **transgressions**.* **Infringement** refers to the encroachment on another's rights: *The lawyer argued that her client's poor treatment was an **infringement** of his rights.*

break   break, crack, split, splinter, shatter

These verbs mean to separate or to cause something to separate into parts or pieces. **Break** is the most general: *Take care not to **break** anything while you're dusting.* **Crack** means to break, often with a sharp snapping sound, without dividing into parts: *We heard the ice **cracking** as we walked on it.* **Split** means to divide along something's length: *These pants have **split** along the seam.* **Splinter** means to split into long, thin, sharp pieces: *Lightning struck the tree and **splintered** it.* **Shatter** means to break into many loose scattered pieces: *The perfume bottle fell and **shattered** on the floor.*

bright   bright, brilliant, radiant, luminous

These adjectives describe something that gives off or reflects light. **Bright** is the most general: ***Bright** sunlight streamed through the window.* **Brilliant** means very bright and shining and often suggests sparkling light: *The treasure chest was full of **brilliant** diamonds.* **Radiant** describes something that gives off or seems to give off light of its own: *I could tell from your **radiant** expression that you had good news to tell me.* **Luminous** is said especially of something that glows in the dark: *Karen's watch has a **luminous** dial.*

Antonym: dark

burn   burn, scorch, char, parch

These verbs mean to injure or change by means of intense heat or flames. **Burn** is the most general: *Dad **burned** some wood in the fireplace to make the room warmer.* **Scorch** means to bring into contact with flame or heated metal and discolor or damage the surface by burning: *I left the iron on by mistake and* ***scorched*** *my new shirt.* ***Char*** means to reduce something to carbon or charcoal by means of fire: *The timbers of the house were* ***charred*** *by the raging fire.* ***Parch*** emphasizes the drying and often fissuring of a surface from exposure to flame, the sun, or hot wind: *The harsh rays of the sun* ***parched*** *the soil.*

business   business, industry, commerce, trade, traffic
These nouns mean activity that produces merchandise.
Business means general commercial, financial, and industrial activity: *This article discusses why American* ***business*** *should invest more in research.* ***Industry*** is the manufacture of goods, especially on a large scale: *The automobile* ***industry*** *has experimented with robots on assembly lines.* ***Commerce*** and ***trade*** both mean the exchange and distribution of goods: *The new economic treaties will have a profound effect on international* ***commerce***. *Those rules don't apply to* ***trade*** *between those countries.* ***Traffic*** often means the business of transporting goods or people: *The city has renovated its harbor to attract shipping* ***traffic***.

calculate   calculate, compute, reckon
These verbs mean to find by using mathematics. ***Calculate*** often suggests something quite complex: *Astronomers know how to* ***calculate*** *the positions of the planets.* ***Compute*** suggests the use of basically straightforward, though possibly lengthy, arithmetic operations: *The bank* ***computes*** *the amount of interest you receive every month.* ***Reckon*** suggests the use of simple arithmetic: *Jan* ***reckoned*** *the number of days left in the school year.*

calm   calm, peaceful, tranquil, placid, serene
These adjectives describe the absence of any disturbance.
Calm and ***peaceful*** mean untroubled in an emotional way: *The other children tried to annoy her, but Charlotte remained* ***calm***. *Which decade was the most* ***peaceful*** *in American history?*

Tranquil describes a more lasting calm: *Howard wanted a* ***tranquil*** *life in the country.* **Placid** means calm in a pleasant, lazy way: *We spent an idle,* ***placid*** *weekend at the shore.* **Serene** means spiritually calm: *It took talent to capture her* ***serene*** *expression in the portrait.*

Antonyms: turbulent, upset

care   care, charge, keeping, trust

These nouns refer to the function of watching, guarding, or overseeing something. *The neighbors left their dog in Gina's* ***care*** *when they went on vacation. Who has* ***charge*** *of collecting today's homework? I left the keys in Dave's* ***keeping***. *The Howells committed their important papers to the bank's* ***trust***.

careful   careful, mindful, observant, watchful

These adjectives mean paying cautious attention. *The children were* ***careful*** *not to get their shoes muddy. Robert was always* ***mindful*** *of his health. Sherlock Holmes is a very* ***observant*** *detective. The* ***watchful*** *clerk noticed you had left your umbrella in the store.*

Antonym: careless

catch   catch, snare, trap

These verbs mean to take in and hold as if by using bait. *The troublemaker ended up* ***caught*** *in her own lies. He found himself* ***snared*** *in the scheme his friends had planned. They were* ***trapped*** *into keeping a promise they had never meant to make.*

center   center, focus, headquarters, hub

These nouns mean a region, person, or thing around which something, such as an activity, is concentrated. *Paris has been considered a great cultural* ***center*** *for hundreds of years. The search for a cure will remain the* ***focus*** *of our experiments. Many corporations have their* ***headquarters*** *in the Midwest. My hometown is the business* ***hub*** *of the whole state.*

chief

chief, principal, main, primary

These adjectives describe what is first in rank or in importance. *Your **chief** responsibility as club secretary is to take notes at our meetings. Vegetables should be a **principal** part of one's diet. What is the **main** theme of the novel? The **primary** function of a house is to provide warmth and shelter.*

choice

choice, alternative, option, preference, selection

These nouns mean the act, power, or right of choosing. ***Choice*** suggests the freedom to choose from a set of things: *It is hard for me to make a **choice** of ice cream flavors at that store because they have so many.* ***Alternative*** means a choice between only two possibilities: *His **alternative** is to take a job he doesn't like or to keep looking for something better.* ***Option*** often means a power to choose that has been granted by someone else: *That school gives you the **option** of taking either art or music instead of study hall.* ***Preference*** means a choice based on one's values, bias, or tastes: *Sheila was offered her **preference** of bright colors.* ***Selection*** suggests a variety of things or persons to choose from: *The director was very careful in the **selection** of actors during auditions.*

clean

clean, cleanly, immaculate, spotless

These adjectives mean free from dirt. *Matt threw the **clean** pair of socks in the hamper by mistake. Cats are generally thought of as **cleanly** animals. The tablecloth was **immaculate** before you spilled juice on it. José made the apartment **spotless** before his guests arrived.*

Antonym: dirty

clear

clear, apparent, obvious, plain

These adjectives mean readily seen, perceived, or understood. *It became **clear** that Sam did not know the right answer. They began laughing for no **apparent** reason. The report has several **obvious** errors in it. The meaning of the teacher's lecture was **plain**: Don't be late!*

---

cold cold, chilly, frigid, frosty, icy

These adjectives describe something at a very low temperature. *The **cold** wind made me wish I had worn a coat. They walked to the store even though the autumn day felt **chilly**. Gordon brought the heater into the **frigid** room. This **frosty** weather is perfect for sledding. The travelers warmed their **icy** hands by the fire.*

Antonym: hot

comfortable comfortable, cozy, snug, restful

These adjectives mean giving ease of mind or body. ***Comfortable*** suggests having no sources of pain or distress: *Tina needs a pair of **comfortable** walking shoes.* ***Cozy*** means homey and reassuring. It brings to mind the image of a warm room in winter: *The puppy curled up in a **cozy** nook near the fireplace.* ***Snug*** makes one think of a secure, cozy shelter: *The children were **snug** in their beds.* ***Restful*** refers to the comfort given by quiet and peace: *Tony spent a **restful** afternoon reading a book.*

comment comment, observation, remark

These nouns mean an expression of fact, opinion, or explanation. *The teacher wrote **comments** in the margins of the report. The reviewer made an interesting **observation** about the movie. Please keep your **remarks** to the topic we're supposed to be discussing.*

common common, ordinary, familiar

These adjectives describe what is generally known or frequently encountered. ***Common*** describes what is customary, takes place often, is widely used, or is well known: *Cavities are a **common** problem for children.* ***Ordinary*** describes what is of the usual kind and is not distinguished in any way from others: *I cooked the rice in the **ordinary** way, so I don't know why it tastes different.* ***Familiar*** describes what is well known or quickly recognized: *The scouts gathered around the campfire and sang old **familiar** songs.*

complete

complete, close, end, conclude

These verbs mean to bring to or come to a stopping point. *Complete* means to bring something to fulfillment: *The students will **complete** their science projects next week.* **Close** means to complete something that has been going on for some time: *The orchestra **closed** the concert with an encore.* **End** emphasizes a definite conclusion: *Many television shows **end** the season with cliffhangers.* **Conclude** can mean to complete or close in a formal way: *The United Nations **concluded** the conference yesterday.*

Antonym: begin

complex

complex, complicated, intricate, involved, knotty

These adjectives mean having parts that are so interconnected that an object or situation is difficult to work with or understand. *Complex* implies a combination of many separate but related parts: *The **complex** instructions for assembling the bicycle consisted of over forty steps.* **Complicated** stresses that the parts have an elaborate relationship: *The social and political factors of the unstable region were so **complicated** that it was almost impossible to develop a plan for peace.* **Intricate** refers to a pattern of intertwining parts that is difficult to follow or study: *The rat was trained to run through an **intricate** maze that had numerous dead-ends.* **Involved** stresses the confusion caused by the blending of parts and the difficulty in separating them: *The reviewer criticized the movie for having **involved** plot twists that were hard to follow.* **Knotty** refers to the something that is difficult to solve or understand: *It took me an hour to solve the **knotty** algebra problem.*

conflict

conflict, contest, combat, fight

These nouns mean a struggle by two or more sides for victory. *Conflict* refers to open fighting between hostile groups as well as an inner struggle between opposing forces: *The mediator tried to resolve the **conflict** between the company's management and the workers.* **Contest** refers to friendly competition or to a hostile struggle to achieve a goal: *Twenty students participated in the spelling* **contest**. **Combat** implies an encounter between two armed persons or groups: *The soldiers on the front lines faced* **combat** *every day*. **Fight** usually refers to a clash involving two opponents: *A* **fight** *was scheduled between the boxing champion and the challenger.*

contain   contain, hold, accommodate

These verbs mean to have within or to have the capacity for having within. **Contain** means to have within or to have as a part: *The movie* **contains** *some funny scenes.* **Hold** stresses capacity for containing: *This pitcher* **holds** *two pints but contains only one because I poured Jason a drink.* **Accommodate** refers to capacity for holding comfortably: *The restaurant* **accommodates** *fifty customers.*

continual   continual, continuous, ceaseless, constant, perpetual

These adjectives mean occurring again and again over a long period of time. **Continual** refers to something that repeats over an interval of time: *The wind caused a* **continual** *banging of the shutter, and it gave me a headache.* **Continuous** and **ceaseless** imply that there is no interruption: *Looking out over the ocean from the beach, the horizon was a* **continuous** *line. The tourists found the* **ceaseless** *thunder of the surf to be soothing.* **Constant** stresses a steady, persistent nature that doesn't change: *The* **constant** *chatter of the monkeys in the zoo was quite loud.* **Perpetual** emphasizes a lack of change over a long period of time: *The lecture was about the* **perpetual** *struggle of good versus evil.*

cruel   cruel, fierce, ferocious, savage

These adjectives mean liking to cause violence, pain, or hardship, or finding satisfaction in the suffering of others. **Cruel** is the most general: *A* **cruel** *tyrant kept the people in constant dread.* **Fierce** suggests the fearless aggression of a wild animal: *Bears are not quite as* **fierce** *as they seem.* **Ferocious** means extremely fierce: *The horror movie features a **ferocious** battle between the monsters.* **Savage** suggests a lack of the control or moderation expected of a civilized person: *You must learn how to overcome your **savage** temper.*

crush

crush, mash, pulp, squash

These verbs mean to press forcefully so as to turn into a pulpy mass. *He stepped on the orange and **crushed** it. I **mashed** the potatoes for our Thanksgiving dinner. Justin **pulped** raspberries through a sieve. Maria **squashed** the grape with the palm of her hand.*

cry

cry, weep, blubber, sob, whimper

These verbs mean to make sounds that show grief, unhappiness, or pain. **Cry** and **weep** both involve the shedding of tears: *Loud, sudden noises make the baby **cry**. No one **wept** at the miser's funeral.* **Blubber** refers to noisy crying mixed with speech that is broken or cannot be understood: *The child **blubbered** over the broken toy.* **Sob** refers to weeping and broken speech marked by gasps: *Stop **sobbing** for a minute and catch your breath!* **Whimper** means to make low, sorrowful, broken cries: *The poor dog came home limping and **whimpering**.*

Antonym: laugh

curious

curious, inquisitive, snoopy, nosy

These adjectives describe persons who show a marked desire for information or knowledge. **Curious** refers to a strong desire to know or learn: *If you are **curious** about a particular subject, the librarian can help you find a book about it.* **Inquisitive** often means too curious: *The **inquisitive** student asked a question every time the teacher paused for breath.* **Snoopy** means curious in a sneaky way: *The **snoopy** reporters searched through the movie star's trash cans for a lead.* **Nosy** means rudely curious: *My **nosy** coworker is always reading other people's mail.*

Antonym: indifferent

dark   dark, dim, murky, dusky, obscure, shady, shadowy

These adjectives describe the absence of light. **Dark** means not lighted enough to see well: *The room was so **dark** I thought there had been a blackout.* **Dim** means so dark that the outlines of things cannot be seen clearly: *I stumbled down the **dim** hallway.* **Murky** means dark as in a smoky or foggy way: *The lighthouse beacon cut through the **murky** air.* **Dusky** describes decreasing light, as at twilight: *Will hurried down the **dusky** streets, trying to get home by dinnertime.* **Shady** describes something sheltered from light, especially sunlight: *We found a **shady** spot in the park for our picnic.* **Shadowy** often describes blocked light or shifting, mysterious shadows: *Sandra shone her flashlight into the **shadowy** well.*

Antonym: light

deceive   deceive, mislead, delude, dupe

These verbs mean to lead another into error, danger, or an unfavorable position:. To **deceive** is to misrepresent the truth on purpose: *The con artist **deceived** the tourist by pretending to be an old friend of the family.* **Mislead** means to lead in the wrong direction or into a mistaken thought or incorrect action: *I was **misled** by the poorly written advertisement into thinking that everything in the store was on sale.* To **delude** is to mislead to the point that a person cannot tell whether something is true or false or cannot make a good judgment: *The chemical company **deluded** the public about the extent of its pollution.* To **dupe** someone is to delude by taking advantage of that person's lack of experience or knowledge: *I was easily **duped** by the corrupt investor because I know nothing about the stock market.*

decide   decide, rule, conclude, resolve

These verbs mean to make or cause to make a decision. **Decide** is the most general: *Kate **decided** to look for a part-time job.* **Rule** suggests that the decision is handed down by someone in authority: *The judge **ruled** that the case should be dismissed.* **Conclude** suggests that a decision, opinion, or judgment has been arrived at after careful consideration: *He **concluded** that it would be better to submit the other poem.* ***Resolve*** stresses the exercise of choice in making a firm decision: *We **resolved** to make the trip no matter what.*

decrease   decrease, lessen, reduce, diminish, dwindle

These verbs mean to become or cause to become smaller or less. ***Decrease*** and ***lessen*** both mean to make smaller or less at a steady, gradual rate: *City traffic **decreases** on holidays. My appetite **lessens** as the weather gets warmer.* ***Reduce*** means to bring down, as in size, degree, or strength: *Maybe you should **reduce** the amount of sugar in the cake recipe.* ***Diminish*** means to decrease by taking away something: *Each new scandal **diminishes** our respect for the senator.* ***Dwindle*** means to decrease bit by bit until no more is left: *Their savings **dwindled** over the years.*

Antonym: add

defeat   defeat, conquer, vanquish, beat

These verbs mean to get the better of an enemy. ***Defeat*** is the most general: *We **defeated** all of the other teams in our division.* ***Conquer*** suggests decisive and often widespread victory: *The Inca **conquered** Peru, Bolivia, and parts of Chile and Ecuador in the fifteenth century.* ***Vanquish*** emphasizes total mastery: *The forces of Napoleon were **vanquished** at Waterloo.* ***Beat*** is less formal than defeat, though it may convey greater emphasis: *Morgan **beats** everyone at chess.*

defend   defend, protect, guard, preserve, shield

These verbs mean to make or keep safe from danger, attack, or harm. ***Defend*** suggests taking measures to drive back an attack: *A small army was formed to **defend** the island against invasion.* ***Protect*** suggests the providing of some kind of cover for safety or comfort: *Wear goggles to **protect** your eyes from the chlorine in the swimming pool.* ***Guard*** means to keep watch over something: *The family bought three big dogs to **guard** the* *house.* **Preserve** means to act to keep something safe: *Ecologists work to **preserve** the balance of nature.* **Shield** means to protect the way armor would, by standing in between the threat and the threatened: *The suspect's lawyers tried to **shield** him from the angry reporters.*

depressed   depressed, blue, dejected, downcast, downhearted

These adjectives mean having low spirits or a sad mood: *Carrie became **depressed** when she lost her job. Miguel felt lonely and **blue** after moving away from his hometown. It was hard not to feel **dejected** when the school newspaper rejected my poem. Everyone on the soccer team looked **downcast** after they lost the game. The students volunteered to go to the nursing home to try to cheer up **downhearted** residents.*

describe   describe, narrate, relate, report

These verbs mean to tell the facts, details, or particulars of something verbally or in writing. *The police officer asked us to **describe** the accident. Ted **narrated** his experiences on the camping trip. The town newspaper **relates** stories of local interest. Melissa came back and **reported** what she had seen.*

desire   desire, crave, want, wish

These verbs mean to feel a strong longing for something. *After long years of fighting, both nations **desire** peace. The young actor went to Hollywood **craving** fame and fortune. Do you **want** to come along? I **wish** summer vacation were here.*

dexterous   dexterous, deft, adroit, handy, nimble

These adjectives refer to skill and ease in performance. **Dexterous** implies physical or mental agility: *The piano player's **dexterous** fingers flew up and down the keyboard.* **Deft** suggests quickness, sureness, neatness, and lightness of touch: *The columnist was known for her **deft** turns of phrase.* **Adroit** implies ease and natural skill, especially in challenging situations: *The **adroit** negotiator hammered out a contract that pleased both* *sides.* **Handy** suggests a more modest ability, principally in manual work: *The carpenter was very **handy** with tools.* **Nimble** stresses quickness and lightness in performing or moving: *Ballet requires a limber body and **nimble** feet.*

dirty   dirty, filthy, foul, grimy

These adjectives apply to what is unclean, impure, or unkempt. **Dirty**, the most general, describes what is covered or stained with dirt: **Dirty** *dishes were piled up in the sink.* **Filthy** means disgustingly dirty: *Put that **filthy** shirt in the washing machine right away.* **Foul** suggests gross offensiveness, particularly to the sense of smell: *A layer of algae covered the **foul** pond.* **Grimy** describes something whose surface is smudged with dirt such as grime or soot: *I found this **grimy** pair of gloves near the gardening tools.*

Antonym: **clean**

disappear   disappear, evaporate, fade, vanish

These verbs mean to pass out of sight or existence. *The small plane **disappeared** in the fog. Dylan's courage **evaporated** when the time came to go to the dentist. As I watched Sara break the record time, my hopes of winning the race **faded** away. No one could figure out how the magician made his assistant **vanish**.*

distribute   distribute, divide, dispense, deal, ration

These verbs mean to give out in portions or shares. **Distribute** is the most general: *In the nineteenth century the United States government **distributed** land to settlers.* **Divide** means to give out portions on the basis of a plan or a purpose: *The estate will be **divided** among the heirs.* **Dispense** often means to give carefully measured or weighed portions: *The clerk **dispensed** the spices carefully.* **Deal** means to distribute in a fair, orderly way: *Each guest was **dealt** a party hat.* **Ration** means to deal out scarce items: *Every household should **ration** water during the drought.*

Antonym: **gather**

easy   easy, simple, effortless, smooth

These adjectives mean requiring little effort. *Easy* describes tasks that are not difficult: *It's **easy** to take care of a pet hamster.* ***Simple*** describes something that is easy because it is not complex: *The best party games have **simple** rules.* ***Effortless*** means seemingly easy because of the strength or skill applied: *The skater performed an **effortless** jump.* ***Smooth*** means free from difficulties or obstacles: *The road to success is hardly ever **smooth**.*

Antonym: difficult

eat   eat, consume, devour

These verbs mean to take food into the body by the mouth. *We **ate** a hearty dinner on Thanksgiving. He greedily **consumed** the sandwich in one bite. Our dog **devours** table scraps with gusto.*

effect   effect, consequence, result, outcome

These nouns mean something, such as an occurrence, a situation, or a condition, that is brought about by a cause. An ***effect*** is produced by the action of an agent or a cause and follows it in time: *What **effect** will your procrastination have?* A ***consequence*** also follows a cause and is traceable to it, but the relationship between them is less sharply definable: *You must accept the **consequences** of your bad choice.* ***Result*** means a final effect, sometimes the last in a series of effects: *What was the **result** of the experiment?* ***Outcome*** means an absolutely final result and may suggest the operation of a cause over a relatively long period: *The **outcome** would have been the same no matter how hard I tried.*

empty   empty, vacant, blank, void, bare

These adjectives describe what contains nothing and therefore lacks what it could have or should have. *Empty* means having no contents or substance: *I thought there were some cherries left, but the bowl was* **empty**. **Vacant** can mean not occupied: *There are many* **vacant** *seats left in the auditorium.* **Blank** means missing something meaningful or important, especially on a surface: *Every poem starts out as a* **blank** *piece of paper.* **Void** means absolutely empty: *The guard's face was* **void** *of all expression.* **Bare** means lacking surface covering or detail. It also means stripped of contents: *The shelves in the store were* **bare** *after the clearance sale.*

Antonym: full

endanger endanger, imperil, jeopardize, risk

These verbs mean to subject to danger, loss, or destruction: *Reckless driving can* **endanger** *people's lives. A camper started a fire that* **imperiled** *the forest. The lengthy strike* **jeopardized** *the company's profits. They* **risked** *their life's savings on questionable stock purchases.*

erase erase, expunge, delete, cancel

These verbs mean to remove or invalidate something, especially something that is stored, recorded, or written down. To **erase** is to wipe or rub out: *I* **erased** *stray marks from the margins before turning in my report.* **Expunge** implies thorough removal: *The assistant* **expunged** *the names of absent students from the list.* To **delete** is to remove matter from a manuscript or data from a computer application: *Elizabeth* **deleted** *the last paragraph from her essay.* **Cancel** refers to invalidating by or as if by drawing lines through something written: *The postal clerk* **cancelled** *the stamp.*

establish establish, create, found, institute

These verbs mean to bring something into existence and set it in operation. *The first public high school for girls in the United States was* **established** *in 1824. Our class* **created** *a scale model of a feudal manor. Scientists hope to* **found** *a colony on Mars someday. The library* **instituted** *a book sale the trustees hoped would become an annual event.*

example   example, case, illustration, sample

Each of these nouns refers to what is representative of or serves to explain something about a larger group or class. An *example* usually shows the character of the whole by representing something of which it is a part: *This is an **example** of typical epic poetry.* **Case** means an action, occurrence, or condition that makes up a specific instance of something being discussed, decided, or treated: *There have been few **cases** of measles this year.* **Illustration** means an example that explains or makes clear: *Make up sentences that are good **illustrations** of the new vocabulary words.* A *sample* is an actual part of something larger, presented as evidence of the quality or nature of the whole: *They are distributing **samples** of a new mouthwash.*

expect   expect, anticipate, hope, await

These verbs have to do with looking ahead to something in the future. *Expect* means to look forward to something that is likely to happen: *Tanya **expects** to get her braces removed next week.* **Anticipate** often means to take advance action, such as to prevent the occurrence of something expected: *I **anticipated** trouble and put the pot roast out of the dog's reach.* **Hope** means to look forward to something with desire and usually to trust that it will actually happen: *We **hope** to see you at the annual meeting.* **Await** means to wait expectantly for something: *I am eagerly **awaiting** your letter.*

expensive   expensive, costly, valuable, priceless

These adjectives apply to what brings a high price or is of great value. *My mother wore an **expensive** silk dress to the banquet. A **costly** Chinese porcelain vase decorated the hall. My parents gave me a **valuable** watch as a graduation present. **Priceless** works of art fill every corner of the museum.*

Antonym: cheap

explain

explain, elucidate, expound, interpret

These verbs mean to make the nature or meaning of something understandable to others. **Explain** is the basic term and has the widest application: *The guide **explained** the meaning of each symbol on the map.* To **elucidate** is to throw light on something difficult: *The teacher **elucidated** the meaning of the nineteenth-century novel so that everyone could understand it.* To **expound** is to give a detailed analysis about a complex subject: *The biology professor **expounded** on the theory of evolution.* To **interpret** is to use special knowledge or insight to reveal the underlying meaning of something: *In a class on film theory, we learned to **interpret** the themes that filmmakers tried to convey.*

fair

fair, just, objective

These adjectives mean free from self-interest, favoritism, or bias in judgment. **Fair** is the most general: *Our gym teacher is respected as a **fair** referee.* **Just** stresses agreement with what is legally or ethically right or proper: *We must reach an agreement that both sides think is **just**.* **Objective** suggests a neutral position that permits observation and judgment without unsuitable reference to one's personal feelings or thoughts: *Try to be **objective** as you listen to the testimony.*

faithful

faithful, loyal, true, steadfast

These adjectives mean adhering firmly and devotedly to someone or something, such as a person, cause, or duty, that elicits or demands one's fidelity. **Faithful** and **loyal** both suggest undeviating attachment. **Loyal** is more often applied to political allegiance: *A dog can be a **faithful** companion. You have proven yourself to be a **loyal** citizen.* **True** suggests steadiness, sincerity, and reliability: *A **true** friend will stand by you.* **Steadfast** strongly suggests fixed, steady loyalty: *Our **steadfast** supporters believed in us from the beginning.*

fashion fashion, style, mode, vogue

These nouns refer to a prevailing or preferred manner of dress, adornment, behavior, or way of life at a given time. *Fashion*, the broadest term, usually refers to what agrees with customs adopted by society or set by artists or intellectuals: *Many magazines include stories on the clothes that are currently in **fashion***. *Style* and *mode* often stress currency or emphasize standards of elegance: *That designer's clothes are always in **style**. Skinny ties were the **mode** in the early 1980s*. *Vogue* often suggests enthusiastic but short-lived acceptance: *Hoop skirts were once in **vogue***.

fast fast, rapid, swift, quick, hasty

These adjectives describe something marked by great speed. *Fast* often describes the person or thing in motion: *You would become a **fast** runner if you stayed in shape*. *Rapid* often describes the activity or movement involved: ***Rapid** advances in technology have changed daily life in a short period of time*. *Swift* describes smoothness and sureness of movement: *Be careful of the **swift** current while you're swimming*. *Quick* usually describes what takes little time: *The driver's **quick** reaction prevented the accident*. *Hasty* describes hurried action and often a lack of care or thought: *The contest judges came to regret their **hasty** decision*.

Antonym: slow

fat fat, pudgy, plump, chubby

These adjectives mean having an abundance and often an excess of flesh. *Fat* implies excessive weight and is generally unfavorable in its connotations: *I must be getting **fat** because my clothes feel tight*. *Pudgy* means short and fat: *Larry played the piano well in spite of his **pudgy** fingers*. *Plump* applies to a pleasing fullness of figure: *A **plump**, rosy-cheeked baby was asleep in the carriage*. *Chubby* means round and plump: *Children often have **chubby** cheeks*.

Antonyms: lean, trim

favorable favorable, propitious, auspicious, conducive

These adjectives describe features that point to a successful outcome. *Favorable* can refer to things that contribute to the reaching of a goal: *Because of the favorable review, the play was sold out every night.* *Propitious* implies a favorable tendency or inclination: *My father was in a good mood, so I figured it was a propitious time to ask for a loan.* *Auspicious* is used of things that indicate success or good fortune: *The project got off to an auspicious start because everyone who was working on it had a lot of experience.* Something *conducive* leads or contributes to a positive or desirable result: *I sat in a quiet place conducive to reading so that I could study.*

fear fear, fright, dread, terror, horror

These nouns refer to the agitation and anxiety caused by the presence or likelihood of danger. *Fear* is the most general term: *She took the train because of her fear of flying.* *Fright* is sudden, usually momentary, great fear: *My friend jumped out from behind the curtain wearing a mask, which gave me quite a fright.* *Dread* is strong fear, especially of something that a person has no power to avoid: *His dread of strangers kept him from leaving his house.* *Terror* is intense overpowering fear: *Years later, the terror of escaping the burning house still gives me nightmares.* *Horror* is a combination of fear and aversion or repulsion: *The horror of the gruesome crime scene sickened the detective.*

feeling feeling, emotion, passion, sentiment

These nouns refer to an intense, complicated mental state such as love or hate. *Feeling* is the most general and neutral: *A feeling of relief washed over the audience when the tightrope walker regained her balance.* *Emotion*, a stronger term, often means an excited or agitated feeling: *The thought of returning home after so many years filled them with emotions.* *Passion* means an intense, compelling emotion: *Getting carried away by passions can lead to serious harm.* *Sentiment* often refers to delicate, sensitive, refined feelings: *Don't let your **sentiments** get the better of you.*

fertile fertile, fruitful, productive, prolific

These adjectives mean marked by great productivity: *The **fertile** farmland yielded corn, soybeans, and wheat. Due to the mayor's **fruitful** efforts, the old railroad line was transformed into a bike trail. During the **productive** meeting, the annual budget was finalized. Dozens of magazines and journals featured the work of the **prolific** writer.*

field field, bailiwick, domain, province, realm

These nouns mean an area of activity, thought, study, or interest: *She is a professor in the **field** of Russian literature. Marketing is his **bailiwick**. Albert Einstein is one of the greatest names in the **domain** of physics. Her newspaper columns cover the **province** of politics. The company hired lawyers who were experts in the **realm** of constitutional law.*

firm firm, hard, solid

These adjectives mean tending not to yield to pressure, touch, or force from the outside. *I would rather sleep on a **firm** mattress. The biscuits I made were as **hard** as granite, even though I thought I had followed the recipe carefully. The parking lot was covered with a **solid** sheet of ice after a night of freezing temperatures.*

flat flat, level, even

These adjectives are applicable to surfaces without irregularities in the form of elevations or depressions. ***Flat*** describes surfaces without curves, bumps, or dents: *It's much easier to write on a **flat** desk.* ***Level*** implies being parallel with the line of the horizon: *We drove past acres of **level** farmland.* ***Even*** refers to flat surfaces in which no part is higher or lower than another: *The water in the pool is as **even** as a mirror.*

follow

follow, succeed, ensue, result

These verbs mean to come after something or someone in time or order. *Follow* is the most general: *I **followed** Brianne to the restaurant because I didn't know the way.* *Succeed* means to follow, especially in a planned order determined by rank, inheritance, or election: *His daughter **succeeded** him as publisher of the local newspaper.* *Ensue* means to follow as an effect or logical development: *If you do not cleanse the wound, an infection may **ensue**.* *Result* means to follow as a direct effect: *Failure to return a library book on time will **result** in a fine.*

foolish

foolish, silly, absurd, ridiculous

These adjectives are applied to what is so devoid of wisdom or good sense as to be laughable. *Foolish*, the least emphatic and derogatory, usually suggests poor judgment or lack of wisdom. It is the least disapproving of these terms: *Tommy's just a **foolish** young fellow, but he'll soon learn his way around.* *Silly* suggests lack of point or purpose: *Amy would have gotten a better grade if she had not made all those **silly** mistakes.* *Absurd* describes something one laughs at because it is unreasonable, illogical, or lacks common sense: *It would be **absurd** for us both to drive, since we're headed for the very same place.* *Ridiculous* describes something that inspires others to make fun of it: *Why are you wearing that **ridiculous** hat?*

Antonym: sensible

forbid

forbid, ban, prohibit

These verbs mean to refuse to allow. *We **forbid** you to chew gum in class. Some airlines have **banned** smoking on all flights. The rules **prohibit** swimming in the reservoir.*

Antonym: allow

forgive

forgive, pardon, excuse, condone

These verbs mean to decide not to punish an offender. *Forgive* means to grant pardon without resentment: *He **forgave** you* *because he knew you didn't mean what you said.* **Pardon** means to free from a penalty: *After the revolution, all political prisoners were **pardoned**.* **Excuse** means to forgive in effect by overlooking a mistake or fault: *Please **excuse** the children for their bad manners.* **Condone** means to excuse an offense, usually a serious one: *I cannot **condone** such horrible behavior by ignoring it.*

frank

frank, candid, outspoken, straightforward

These adjectives mean revealing or apt to reveal one's thoughts freely and honestly: **Frank** implies directness, often bluntly so: *The instructor was **frank** and told me exactly why I was failing the class.* **Candid** refers to the refusal to evade difficult or unpleasant issues: *In a **candid** conversation with my counselor, I learned that I have low self-esteem.* **Outspoken** implies a bold lack of reserve: *The **outspoken** activist demanded to speak to the mayor.* **Straightforward** refers to a direct of manner and expression: *My teacher was **straightforward** and told me that I had to study harder.*

frighten

frighten, scare, alarm, terrify, panic

These verbs mean to cause fear in someone or something. **Frighten** is the most general: *It's hard to believe that elephants are **frightened** of mice.* **Scare** is also general, but less formal: *Don't let the amount of homework **scare** you.* **Alarm** means to frighten suddenly: *A loss of ten pounds in a month **alarmed** her doctor.* **Terrify** means to overwhelm with fear: *We were **terrified** that the footbridge would collapse as we walked on it.* **Panic** means to alarm someone to the point of losing self-control: *False reports of an invasion **panicked** the whole city.*

funny

funny, comical, humorous, laughable

These adjectives mean causing amusement or laughter. *Dan tells the **funniest** jokes. We performed a **comical** routine at the school talent show. Tell us a **humorous** story to cheer us up. Which was more **laughable**, the sack race or the egg toss?*

Antonym: serious

gather

gather, collect, assemble, accumulate

These verbs mean to bring together in a group or mass. *Gather* is the most general: *I gathered sticks to build a fire.* *Collect* often means to select like or related things that then become part of an organized whole: *Many people like to collect stamps and coins from around the world.* *Assemble* means to gather persons or things that have a definite and usually close relationship: *The curator is assembling Stone Age artifacts to make an interesting exhibit.* *Accumulate* describes the increase of like or related things over an extended period of time: *We accumulated piles of old newspapers in the basement.*

glad

glad, happy, cheerful, lighthearted, joyful

These adjectives mean being in or showing good spirits. *Glad* often means satisfied with immediate circumstances: *I am so glad we finally met.* *Happy* can mean feeling pleasurable contentment, as from a sense of fulfillment: *Jane is happy with her new job.* *Cheerful* means having good spirits, as from being pleased: *Leroy tried to remain cheerful while he was in the hospital.* *Lighthearted* means free of cares and worries: *Summertime always puts you in a lighthearted mood.* *Joyful* means having great happiness and liveliness: *Their wedding was a joyful occasion.*

Antonym: sad

guide

guide, lead, shepherd, steer, usher

These verbs mean to conduct on the way or direct to the way. *We were guided to our seats. The teacher led the students in a discussion of the novel's themes. The tourists were shepherded to the chartered bus. The secretary steered the applicant to the proper department. The host will now usher the contestants into a soundproof booth.*

habit

habit, practice, custom

These nouns refer to a pattern of behavior established by repetition. *Habit* means a way of acting that has been repeated so many times it no longer involves conscious thought: *Paula has a **habit** of covering her mouth when she laughs.* **Practice** means a routine, often chosen way of acting: *It is their **practice** to eat dinner early.* **Custom** means a usually longstanding practice in line with social conventions: *It is a Japanese **custom** not to wear shoes in the house.*

happen

happen, chance, occur

These verbs mean to come about. *What would **happen** if you refused? It **chanced** that we succeeded. The accident **occurred** recently.*

harass

harass, harry, hound, pester

These verbs mean to trouble persistently or incessantly. ***Harass*** and ***harry*** imply persistent annoyance or persecution by bothering, threatening, or demanding something from someone repeatedly: *The landlord **harassed** tenants who were behind in their rent. The rude customer **harried** the clerk.* ***Hound*** suggests unrelenting pursuit to gain a desired goal or end: *Reporters and photographers **hounded** the celebrity.* To ***badger*** is to nag or tease persistently: *The children **badgered** their parents for new toys.* To ***pester*** is to inflict a succession of petty annoyances: *My younger brother continued to **pester** me by asking me silly questions.*

healthy

healthy, sound, robust, well, hardy

These adjectives refer to good physical or mental health. ***Healthy*** stresses the absence of disease: *The coach encouraged us to eat nutritious foods so that we would be **healthy**.* ***Sound*** indicates freedom from injury or impairment: *When you write a will you must be of **sound** mind.* ***Robust*** refers to strength and ruggedness: *The **robust** soldiers marched for ten hours.* ***Well*** indicates that a person is not sick or has recovered from a sickness: *My grandfather was in the hospital, but he's back home now that he's **well**.* ***Hardy*** refers to being in good health along with the ability to withstand harsh or difficult conditions: *The **hardy** hikers finally reached the summit of the mountain after a difficult climb.*

heap
heap, mound, pile, stack

These nouns mean a group or collection of things lying one on top of the other. *Their toys lay in a **heap** on the floor. **Mounds** of boulders dotted the construction site. You'll find a **pile** of boxes in the garage. He kept a **stack** of firewood beside the front door.*

heavy
heavy, weighty, hefty, massive

These adjectives mean having a relatively great weight. ***Heavy*** and ***weighty*** refer to what has great weight: *That load is too **heavy** to lift. What could be inside such a **weighty** package?* ***Hefty*** refers principally to physical heaviness or brawniness: *The tall, **hefty** wrestler entered the ring.* ***Massive*** describes what is bulky, heavy, solid, and strong: ***Massive** marble columns still stood among the ruins.*

Antonym: light

help
help, aid, assist

These verbs mean to contribute to fulfilling a need, furthering an effort, or achieving a purpose. ***Help*** and ***aid*** are the most general: *A new medicine has been developed to **help** (or **aid**) digestion.* ***Help*** often means to aid in an active way: *I'll **help** you move the sofa.* ***Assist*** often means to play a secondary role in aiding: *A few of the students **assisted** the professor in researching the data.*

hide
hide, conceal, secrete, screen, bury

These verbs mean to keep from the sight or knowledge of others. ***Hide*** and ***conceal*** are the most general: *She smiled to **hide** her hurt feelings. A throw rug **concealed** the stain on the carpet.* ***Secrete*** means to hide in a place unknown to others: *The lioness **secreted** her cubs in the tall grass.* ***Screen*** means to shield or block from the view of others: *Tall shrubs **screen** the* *actor's home from inquisitive tourists.* **Bury** means to conceal something by covering it over: *He **buried** his hands in his pockets so the teacher couldn't see his dirty fingernails.*

hurry

hurry, haste, speed

These nouns mean rapidity or promptness of movement or activity. *They worked carefully without any **hurry**. The unmasked spy left the room in **haste**. David and Joe cleaned up the whole apartment with remarkable **speed**.*

hurt

hurt, injure, damage, spoil

These verbs mean to affect in a bad way. **Hurt** can mean to cause pain, distress, or loss: *Don't try to lift the heavier boxes because you might **hurt** your back.* **Injure** can mean to harm health, well-being, appearance, or expectations: *Linda didn't want a heavy lunch to **injure** her chances of winning the race.* **Damage** can mean to injure in a way that decreases value or usefulness: *The movers must have **damaged** the piano because I never noticed that dent before now.* **Spoil** means to damage something so that its value, excellence, or strength is ultimately destroyed: *The heavy rains and wind **spoiled** our picnic.*

Antonyms: heal, help, improve

idea

idea, thought, notion, concept

These nouns mean something formed or represented in the mind, a product of mental activity. **Idea** is the most general: *Writers sometimes have many **ideas** before they begin work.* **Thought** can mean an idea produced by contemplation and reason as opposed, for example, to emotion: *The **thoughts** of great philosophers are worth our attention.* **Notion** means a vague, general, or even fanciful idea: *Max has a **notion** to travel around Europe someday.* **Concept** means an idea on a large scale: *He seems to have a profound **concept** of time.*

ideal

ideal, model, example

These nouns can refer to someone or something worthy of imitation or duplication. *You can find inspiration in your* **ideals**. *Gloria is a* **model** *of what a student should be. The best teachers teach by their* **example**.

imitate

imitate, copy, mimic, simulate

These verbs mean to follow something or someone as a model. ***Imitate*** means to act like another or follow a pattern set by another: *I tried to* **imitate** *a British accent.* ***Copy*** means to duplicate an original as closely as possible: *If you were absent,* **copy** *the notes from a classmate.* ***Mimic*** often means to imitate in order to make fun of someone or something: *The class clown got caught* **mimicking** *the teacher.* ***Simulate*** means to falsely take on the appearance or character of something: *They painted the wall to* **simulate** *marble.*

importance

importance, consequence, significance

These nouns refer to the state or quality of being significant, influential, or worthy of note or esteem. ***Importance*** is the most general term: *It isn't wise to ignore the* **importance** *of exercise and a proper diet to staying fit and healthy.* ***Consequence*** refers to importance that has to do with outcome, result, or effect: *They have not made any changes of* **consequence**. ***Significance*** refers to the quality of something, often not obvious, that gives it special meaning or value: *Your vote can be of real* **significance** *in the outcome of the election.*

increase

increase, expand, enlarge, extend, multiply

These verbs mean to become or make greater or larger. ***Increase***, the most general, often means to grow steadily: *The number of students here has* **increased** *every year since 1975.* ***Expand*** means to increase in size, volume, or amount: *The pizza parlor* **expanded** *its delivery service to cover a wider area.* ***Enlarge*** means to make larger: *Sue likes that photograph so* much that she wants to **enlarge** and frame it. **Extend** means to increase in length: *The transit authority* **extended** *the subway line to the suburbs.* **Multiply** means to increase in number: *One of the zoo's roles is to help endangered species* **multiply**.

Antonym: decrease

intention   intention, intent, purpose, goal, end, aim, object

These nouns refer to what one plans to do or achieve. **Intention** signifies a course of action that one proposes to follow: *It is my* **intention** *to take a vacation next month.* **Intent** more strongly implies deliberate thoughts or plans: *The executor complied with the testator's* **intent**. **Purpose** strengthens the idea of resolution or determination: *The* **purpose** *of this class is to teach you how to swim.* **Goal** may suggest an idealistic or long-term purpose: *The charity set a* **goal** *to raise ten million dollars.* **End** suggests a long-range goal: *The dictator would use any means possible to achieve that* **end**. **Aim** stresses the direction one's efforts take in pursuit of an end: *The* **aim** *of most students is to graduate.* An **object** is an end that one tries to carry out: *The* **object** *of chess is to capture your opponent's king.*

interesting   interesting, intriguing, fascinating, engaging

These adjectives mean capable of capturing and holding one's attention. *You may write your report on any subject you find* **interesting**. *Sue thought my idea was* **intriguing** *and wanted to know more about it. It's* **fascinating** *that lasers can be used to perform surgery! All the characters in the play are* **engaging**.

Antonym: dull

interfere   interfere, meddle, tamper

These verbs mean to influence or affect the affairs of others when unasked to do so, especially in an irritating or improper way. **Interfere** suggests action that seriously harms or frustrates: *I wish you wouldn't* **interfere** *in my private matters.* **Meddle** can suggest unwanted, unwarranted, or unnecessary

intrusion: *Stop **meddling** in things that don't concern you.*
Tamper means to interfere by making changes that are unwelcome and often destructive or by trying to influence another in an improper way: *George **tampered** with their books and papers and got everything out of order.*

jerk

jerk, snap, wrench, yank

These verbs mean to move with a sudden short, quick motion: *The sailor **jerked** the rope twice to pull it taut. The lawyer **snapped** shut the lock of her briefcase. She **wrenched** the stick out of my hand. He **yanked** the door open with a tug.*

join

join, combine, unite, link, connect

These verbs mean to fasten or attach two or more things together. ***Join*** can mean to bring separate things together physically: *We **joined** the pipes together and turned on the water.* ***Combine*** often means to mix or merge different things for a specific purpose: *Jason **combined** oil, vinegar, and herbs to make a salad dressing.* ***Unite*** suggests the joining of separate parts into a thoroughly blended whole with its own identity: *The prince **united** the little kingdoms to form a large nation.* ***Link*** and ***connect*** can mean to attach firmly without taking away the special characteristics of each part: *The train's engine and cars are **linked** together with strong bolts. The new tunnel under the English Channel **connects** Great Britain and France.*

Antonyms: separate, divide

joke

joke, jest, gag

These nouns mean something that is said or done for laughter or amusement. ***Joke*** especially means an amusing story with a punch line at the end: *He tells the most hilarious **jokes**.* ***Jest*** suggests playful humor: *Yes, I said it, but only as a **jest**.* ***Gag*** is principally applicable to a broadly comic remark, act, or trick: *Who thought of the best **gag** for April Fools' Day?*

judge

judge, arbitrator, arbiter, referee, umpire

These nouns refer to persons who make decisions that determine or settle points that are at issue. A **judge** is a person capable of making rational, dispassionate, and wise decisions: *In this case, the jury members are the **judges** of the truth.* An **arbitrator** is either appointed or derives authority from the consent of people who are in dispute: *An experienced **arbitrator** mediated the contract dispute.* An **arbiter** is a person whose opinion or judgment is recognized as being unassailable or binding: *The critic considered himself an **arbiter** of fine literature.* **Referee** and **umpire** usually refer to sports officials who enforce the rules and settle points at issue: *The **referee** blew his whistle to signal the end of the game. The **umpire** ruled that the pitch was a strike.*

keep

keep, retain, withhold, reserve

These verbs mean to maintain something in one's possession or control. **Keep** is the most general: *Sometimes it's easier to earn money than to **keep** it.* **Retain** means to continue to hold something, especially when in danger of losing it: *No matter what goes wrong, Sarah manages to **retain** her sense of humor.* **Withhold** means to refuse to give or allow: *The tenants **withheld** their rent until the landlord made repairs.* **Reserve** means to hold for future use: *Please **reserve** your questions for the discussion period.*

knowledge

knowledge, information, learning

These nouns refer to what is known, as by having been gotten through study or experience. **Knowledge**, the broadest term, includes facts and ideas, understanding, and the totality of what is known: *He has a good, general **knowledge** of many different subjects.* **Information** often suggests a collection of facts and data: *I can't make a decision until I have all the **information** on the case.* **Learning** usually means knowledge that is gained by schooling and study: *Her **learning** is amazing considering how young she is.*

large

large, big, enormous, great, huge

These adjectives mean notably above the average in size or magnitude. *Los Angeles is a **large** city. Factory outlet stores usually offer **big** discounts. A computer can store an **enormous** amount of information. I'd like to take a cruise on a **great** ocean liner. Everyone had **huge** helpings of potato salad at the picnic.*

Antonym: small

last

last, final, ultimate

These adjectives mean coming after all others in order. ***Last*** applies to what comes at the end of a series, as of like things: *Our club meets on the **last** day of the month.* Something ***final*** comes at the end of a series or process and stresses a definite and decisive conclusion: *This is our **final** offer.* ***Ultimate*** means final and often describes something distant or remote, as in time: *Our **ultimate** goal is to be self-employed.*

Antonym: first

lean

lean, thin, slender, spare, skinny, scrawny

These adjectives mean having little or no excess flesh. ***Lean*** means lacking fat: ***Leaner** cuts of meat are better for your health.* ***Thin*** and ***slender*** mean having a lean body: *It's amazing how you can drink a milk shake every day and stay **thin**. A century ago, heavier builds were considered more beautiful than **slender** ones.* ***Spare*** often means trim with good muscle tone: *She has the **spare** figure of a marathon runner.* ***Skinny*** and ***scrawny*** mean unattractively thin, as if undernourished: *The boy had **skinny**, freckled legs with prominent knees. If you exercise more instead of dieting you won't look so **scrawny**.*

Antonym: fat

lift

lift, raise, hoist, heave, boost

These verbs mean to move something from a lower to a higher level or position. ***Lift*** sometimes stresses the effort involved: *The trunk proved too heavy to **lift**.* ***Raise*** often suggests movement to a more or less vertical position: *They **raised** the drawbridge so that the invaders could not cross the moat.* ***Hoist*** mostly refers to lifting heavy objects, often by mechanical means: *Have they considered **hoisting** the sunken ship out of the water?* ***Heave*** means to lift or raise with great effort or force: *Bob **heaved** the pack onto his back.* ***Boost*** suggests lifting by pushing from below: *She **boosted** the child onto the pony's saddle.*

little

little, small, miniature, tiny, wee

These adjectives mean notably below average in size. *I am knitting a **little** blanket for the baby. The house would be too **small** for a large family, but it's perfect for newlyweds. Grandmother served delicious **miniature** cakes at teatime. The recipe calls for a **tiny** pinch of baking powder. Dan feels a **wee** bit better now that he has had some rest.*

Antonym: big

look

look, watch, gaze

These verbs mean to use the eyes to see, especially with care or attention. ***Look*** and ***watch*** are general terms: *I **looked** at the pictures on the wall. We **watch** the fireworks every year.* ***Gaze*** means to look steadily for a long time: *He relaxed by the fireplace, **gazing** into the flames.*

love

love, like, enjoy, relish, fancy

These verbs mean to be attracted to or to find agreeable. ***Love*** means to feel a strong emotional attachment or intense affection for: *They **love** their cat as if it were a member of the family.* ***Like***, a less forceful word, means to be interested in, to approve of, or to favor something: *Erica **likes** her new school much better than the old one.* ***Enjoy*** means to feel personal satisfaction or pleasure from: *I would have **enjoyed** the movie more if the people behind me hadn't been talking so loudly.* ***Relish*** means to appreciate keenly or zestfully: *They always **relish** hearing a good joke.* ***Fancy*** means to find something appealing to one's taste or imagination: *Elvis **fancied** big, flashy cars.*

Antonyms: dislike, hate

magnificent

magnificent, grand, majestic, imposing, grandiose

These adjectives mean very large and impressive. ***Magnificent*** means marked by luxurious splendor and grandeur: *The Taj Mahal is a **magnificent** example of architecture.* ***Grand*** and ***majestic*** suggest lofty dignity or nobility: *The President welcomed the foreign officials with a **grand** ceremony. The mountain climbers struggled up the **majestic** slopes of the Alps.* ***Imposing*** means impressive because of size, bearing, or power: *We stared up at the **imposing** statue of Abraham Lincoln.* ***Grandiose*** can often mean imposing in a pompous, pretentious, or otherwise negative way: *The politician's **grandiose** speech about world peace turned out to be nothing but empty words.*

margin

margin, border, edge, brink, rim

These nouns mean the line or narrow area that marks the outside limit of something. ***Margin*** means an outside area that is different somehow from the inside: *Cornflowers grow along the **margin** of the meadow.* ***Border*** can mean a boundary line: *The farmer built a fence along the **border** of the property.* ***Edge*** can mean the precise bounding line where two different surfaces meet: *Mark curled his toes over the **edge** of the diving board.* ***Brink*** means the upper edge of something steep: *The car teetered on the **brink** of the canyon.* ***Rim*** often means the edge of something that is circular or curved: *There is a small nick in the **rim** of the telescope lens.*

mark

mark, label, tag, ticket

These verbs mean to place a mark of identification on. *We **marked** the items for sale at the auction. We need to **label** the boxes on the shelf before mailing them. Did you remember to **tag** the suitcases with your name and address? They **ticketed** the new merchandise this morning.*

method

method, system, routine, manner

These nouns refer to the plans or procedures followed to accomplish a task or reach a goal. *Method* suggests a detailed, logically ordered plan: *Greg developed a **method** for finishing his homework in half the time.* *System* means a coordinated group of methods: *Their **system** of doing experiments was well worked out.* *Routine* means a habitual, often tiresome method: *His **routine** for cleaning the house never changes.* *Manner* means a personal or distinctive method of action: *I'm probably the only one with my **manner** of tying knots.*

mix

mix, blend, merge, fuse, mingle

These verbs mean to put into or come together in one mass. *Mix* is the most general term: *Julie **mixed** the blue and yellow paints together on her palette.* *Blend* means to mix thoroughly so that the parts lose their separate characteristics: *They **blend** coffee and cocoa beans together to make a special mocha drink.* *Merge* means to absorb one thing into another to make a new whole: *Two different rivers **merge** to form the Nile.* *Fuse* means to make a strong union by merging: *Rust had **fused** the screw to the metal.* *Mingle* often means to mix without changing the component parts: *They **mingled** the vinegar and oil in the bowl.*

Antonym: separate

mixture

mixture, blend, compound, composite

These nouns refer to a combination produced by mixing. *Mixture* has the widest application: *The cookie batter was a **mixture** of flour, sugar, and eggs.* *Blend* implies that the original components have lost their distinctness: *The novel is a fascinating **blend** of romance and realism.* A *compound* constitutes a new and independent entity: *The school's program is a **compound** of scholarship and athleticism.* A *composite* has components that may retain part of their identities: *The suite is a **composite** of themes for various parts of the opera.*

moment
moment, instant, jiffy, flash

These nouns mean a short interval of time. ***Moment*** means a short but not insignificant period of time: *I'll be with you in a **moment**.* ***Instant*** is a period of time almost too short to notice: *She paused for just an **instant**.* *In a **jiffy*** means in a short space of time, while *in a **flash*** suggests the almost unnoticeable length of time of a flash of light: *I will be off the computer in a **jiffy**. She was on her feet in a **flash** when the bell rang.*

mood
mood, humor, temper

These nouns can refer to a temporary state of mind or feeling. ***Mood*** is the most general term: *The principal seems to be in a cheerful **mood** today.* ***Humor*** often suggests a state of mind resulting from one's characteristic way of thinking or acting, sometimes suggesting restlessness or change: *The **humor** of the lecturer changed as half the audience walked out.* ***Temper*** most often means a state of mind marked by irritability or strong anger: *You were in such a **temper** everyone was afraid to come near you.*

muscular
muscular, athletic, brawny, burly, sinewy

These adjectives mean strong and powerfully built. *I lift weights because I want a more **muscular** body. The **athletic** young woman won all the races at the company picnic. They need some **brawny** friends to help move that piano. The wharf was crowded with **burly** men waiting to unload the ship's cargo. Professional dancers are usually lean and **sinewy**.*

Antonym: scrawny

mysterious
mysterious, esoteric, arcane, occult

These adjectives mean beyond human power to explain or understand. Something ***mysterious*** arouses wonder and inquisitiveness and also eludes comprehension: *The authorities were unable to explain the **mysterious** glow that surrounded the cave.* What is ***esoteric*** is mysterious because only a small select group of people knows and understands it: *The obscure* *literary journal was a compilation of* **esoteric** *philosophical essays.* **Arcane** applies to what is hidden from the knowledge of everyone except those people who have the key to a secret: *Few investors actually understand those* **arcane** *economic theories.* **Occult** suggests knowledge reputedly gained only by secret, magical, or supernatural means: *The historian studied* **occult** *rites practiced during the Middle Ages.*

naive

naive, simple, unsophisticated, guileless

These adjectives mean free from guile, cunning, or sham. **Naive** sometimes connotes a credulity that gets in the way of functioning effectively in a practical world: *The car salesman took advantage of the* **naive** *customer.* **Simple** stresses absence of complexity, artifice, pretentiousness, or dissimulation: *The novelist wrote* **simple**, *unadorned prose that was accessible to a wide audience.* **Unsophisticated** indicates absence of worldliness: *The* **unsophisticated** *tourists were shocked that their hotel room didn't have air conditioning.* **Guileless** signifies absence of insidious or treacherous cunning: *The innocent child had a harmless,* **guileless** *gaze.*

nautical

nautical, marine, maritime, naval

These adjectives mean of or relating to the sea, ships, shipping, sailors, or navigation. **Nautical** *charts show where there are underwater rocks. We studied* **marine** *plants and animals on our field trip to the shore. I'm reading about the* **maritime** *history of the American colonies. The* **naval** *officer issued a statement to the media about the warships.*

neat

neat, tidy, trim, shipshape

These adjectives mean marked by good order and cleanliness. **Neat** means pleasingly clean and orderly: *Marcia pulled back her hair into a* **neat** *ponytail.* **Tidy** suggests precise arrangement and order: *Even their closets and drawers were kept* **tidy**. **Trim** stresses a smart appearance because of neatness, tidiness, and pleasing proportions: *The* **trim** *little boat was all ready to* *set sail.* **Shipshape** means both neat and tidy: *We'll have the kitchen* **shipshape** *in no time.*

Antonyms: messy, sloppy

new

new, fresh, novel, newfangled, original

These adjectives describe what has existed for only a short time or has only lately come into use or gained importance. **New** is the most general: *Jerry made a lot of* **new** *friends at camp.* **Fresh** means new and lively, bright, or pure: *Identifying the virus gave scientists* **fresh** *hope of discovering a vaccine.* **Novel** describes what is both new and strikingly unusual: *We are seeking* **novel** *ways to produce energy.* **Newfangled** suggests that something is unnecessarily novel: *He's always buying some* **newfangled** *gadget.* **Original** describes something novel and the first of its kind: *This is my own* **original** *idea.*

Antonym: old

normal

normal, regular, typical

These adjectives mean not different from what is common, usual, or to be expected. **Normal** stresses agreement with an established standard, model, or pattern: *Your forehead feels hot, but your body temperature is* **normal**. **Regular** often stresses agreement with a fixed rule or principle or a uniform procedure: **Regular** *attendance in class is required.* **Typical** stresses harmony with those qualities, traits, or characteristics that identify a kind, group, or category: *A* **typical** *summer day in Arizona is hot and dry.*

noted

noted, celebrated, famous, illustrious, renowned

These adjectives mean widely known and esteemed. *Our library has invited a* **noted** *author to read from her new book. The concert series features many* **celebrated** *musicians. The* **famous** *scientist wrote an article discussing computers and robots. An* **illustrious** *judge presided over the case. The* **renowned** *actor lent some credibility to the new movie project.*

Antonyms: unknown, obscure

obligation obligation, responsibility, duty

These nouns refer to a course of action demanded of a person, as by law or conscience, for example. *Obligation* usually refers to a specific pressure caused by something in particular: *Parents have an **obligation** to take care of their children. **Responsibility** stresses being accountable for fulfilling an obligation: It is your **responsibility** to walk the dog after school. **Duty** refers especially to responsibility that a person feels because of one's morals or ethics: The students volunteered out of a sense of **duty**.*

obstinate obstinate, stubborn, mulish, headstrong

These adjectives mean determinedly unwilling to yield. *Obstinate* means unreasonably rigid and difficult to persuade: *Jenny is **obstinate** about doing things in her own way. **Stubborn** and **mulish** can mean perversely unyielding by nature: Robert is too **stubborn** to admit that he was wrong. It's **mulish** of you to refuse to look at the map until after we're lost. **Headstrong** means stubbornly, often recklessly willful: That **headstrong** child is always getting into trouble but will never follow advice.*
Antonyms: **cooperative, flexible**

occurrence occurrence, event, incident, circumstance

These nouns refer to something that takes place or comes to pass. *Occurrence* is the most general: *The rising of the sun is an everyday **occurrence**. **Event** usually signifies a notable occurrence: The Indianapolis 500 is a major racing **event** that takes place every year. An **incident** refers to a distinct event of sharp identity and significance: A political assassination was the **incident** that sparked the beginning of World War I. **Circumstance** denotes a particular incident or occurrence: The presence of security guards was a fortunate **circumstance**, because they were able to prevent the robbery from taking place.*

offend offend, insult, outrage

These verbs mean to cause resentment, humiliation, or hurt. *Offend* means to cause displeasure, wounded feelings, or disgust in another: *I hope I haven't **offended** you by speaking so carelessly.* **Insult** suggests gross insensitivity, lack of respect, or contemptuous rudeness that causes shame or embarrassment: *She walked away when they began to **insult** her.* **Outrage** implies the outright violation of a person's integrity, pride, or sense of right and decency: *He was **outraged** when the neighbors refused to band together to help fight crime in the neighborhood.*

old

old, ancient, obsolete, antique

These adjectives describe what belongs to or dates from an earlier time or period. **Old** is the most general term: *We found a box full of **old** records in the attic.* **Ancient** refers to the distant past: *Mesopotamia was the site of an **ancient** civilization.* **Obsolete** describes something that is no longer used: *It is time to replace that **obsolete** machine with a newer model.* **Antique** refers both to what is very old and to what is especially appreciated or valued because of its age: *She collects **antique** furniture and clothing.*

Antonym: modern

oppose

oppose, fight, combat, contest, resist

These verbs mean to try to overcome, defeat, or turn back someone or something. **Oppose** is the most general: *They **opposed** the plan to shut down the factory.* **Fight** and **combat** mean to oppose in an aggressive or active way: *Citizens must work together to **fight** corruption in government. The development of vaccines was an important step toward **combating** disease.* **Contest** means to call something into question and take an active stand against it: *The losing candidate **contested** the election.* **Resist** means to turn aside or counteract the actions, effects, or force of someone or something: *The provinces united to **resist** the invasion.*

Antonym: support

origin

origin, source, root

These nouns mean the point at which something begins. **Origin** can mean the point at which something comes into existence: *We can trace the **origin** of that theory*. ***Source*** means the point from which something comes or springs into being: *Ancient myths can still be a **source** of inspiration for writers*. ***Root*** often means the fundamental cause of something or basic reason for something: *They need to get at the **root** of the problem*.

outline   outline, contour, profile, silhouette

These nouns refer to a line that defines the boundary and shape of an object, mass, or figure: *The **outline** of the mountains against the sunset was a majestic sight. She could see the island's **contour** from the airplane. This ancient coin features the **profile** of a king. From the train, he saw the dark **silhouette** of his family waving farewell on the platform*.

pacify   pacify, mollify, appease, placate

These verbs refer to allaying another's anger, belligerence, discontent, or agitation. To ***pacify*** is to restore calm to or establish peace in: *The babysitter **pacified** the baby by giving her a bottle of milk*. ***Mollify*** stresses the soothing of hostile feelings: *The therapist **mollified** the angry teenager by speaking gently*. ***Appease*** and ***placate*** suggest the satisfaction of claims or demands or the tempering of antagonism, often by concessions: *I **appeased** my friend's anger with a compliment. An apology from the clerk **placated** the indignant customer*.

pamper   pamper, indulge, spoil, coddle, baby

These verbs mean to make ridiculous or excessive efforts to please someone. ***Pamper*** means to satisfy someone's appetites, tastes, or desires: *I **pampered** myself with a long hot bath*. ***Indulge*** means to yield to wishes or impulses, especially those which would be better left unfulfilled: *The twins **indulged** their craving for sweets by sharing a banana split*. ***Spoil*** means to indulge someone in a way that worsens his or her character: *You are **spoiling** that child, letting him have every toy he wants*. ***Coddle*** means to care for in a tender, overprotective way that can weaken character: *Don't **coddle** her and make her think she can't do the job all by herself.* **Baby** suggests giving someone the kind of attention one might give a baby: *Michael likes to be **babied** when he has the flu.*

Antonyms: punish, abuse

pause

pause, intermission, recess, suspension

These nouns mean a temporary stop in activity. *There was a brief **pause** in the conversation. They planned to serve punch during the play's **intermission**. Enjoy yourselves during the winter **recess**. The strike caused a **suspension** of repair work on the highway.*

perfect

perfect, faultless, flawless, impeccable

These adjectives mean without any defects or errors. *I think I have found the **perfect** solution. The lecturer argued her point with **faultless** logic. That museum owns the largest **flawless** gem in the world. They spoke **impeccable** French after spending several years in the south of France.*

perform

perform, execute, accomplish, achieve, fulfill

These verbs mean to carry through to completion. ***Perform*** means to carry out an action, an undertaking, or a technique. The word often suggests observance of due form or the exercise of skill or care: *Sophisticated laser experiments are **performed** regularly in the laboratory.* **Execute** suggests performing a task or putting something into effect by following a plan or design: *Greg **executed** the difficult dive perfectly.* **Accomplish** suggests the successful completion of something, often of something that requires determination or talent: *You can **accomplish** anything you set your mind to.* **Achieve** means to accomplish something especially through effort or despite difficulty. The term often suggests an important result: *They **achieved** success through hard work and dedication.* **Fulfill** means to live up to expectations or satisfy demands, wishes, or requirements: *The exciting trip **fulfilled** her lifelong dream of traveling across country by train.*

pity

pity, compassion, sympathy

These nouns mean kindly concern awakened by the bad luck, hardship, or suffering of another. *Pity* often suggests a feeling of sorrow that makes one want to help or to show mercy: *He feels no **pity** for his enemies.* **Compassion** means deep awareness of the suffering of another and the wish to relieve it: *The best doctors treat their patients with **compassion**. **Sympathy** refers to sharing in the sorrows or troubles of another: *I can't do anything to help you, but you have my **sympathy**.*

plan

plan, design, project, scheme, strategy

These nouns mean a method or program that is thought out to guide one in doing something. *Tom has no vacation **plans** yet. The car manufacturers published their **designs** of next year's models. I have several **projects** for my spring vacation. We're coming up with a new **scheme** to save energy. What **strategy** will you use at this point in the chess game?*

polite

polite, mannerly, civil, courteous

These adjectives mean mindful of, conforming to, or marked by good manners. ***Polite*** and ***mannerly*** mean considerate of others and well-bred according to social standards: *You don't have to like all your relatives, but you must be **polite** to them. Are rural people really more **mannerly** than city dwellers?* **Civil** means having a minimal amount of good manners, neither polite nor rude: *He is barely **civil** until he has his morning coffee.* **Courteous** means polite in a gracious, courtly way: *She wrote a **courteous** response accepting their invitation.*

Antonym: **rude**

praise

praise, acclaim, commend, extol

These verbs mean to express approval or admiration. **Praise** is the most general: *The teacher **praised** her students whenever they did a good job.* **Acclaim** usually implies hearty praise that is warmly and publicly expressed: *Critics from major newspapers **acclaimed** the new film very highly.* **Commend** suggests moderate or restrained approval, as from a superior: *The judge* **commended** *the jury for their work.* **Extol** suggests exaltation or glorification: *The preacher* **extolled** *the virtue of charity.*

prevent

prevent, preclude, avert, obviate, forestall

These verbs mean to stop or hinder something from happening, especially by planning or acting in advance. **Prevent** is the most general: *The bars over the windows* **prevent** *people from breaking into the apartment.* To **preclude** is to exclude the possibility of an event or action: *Regularly brushing your teeth with fluoridated toothpaste should* **preclude** *the formation of cavities.* To **avert** is to ward off something about to happen: *Thanks to the pilot's quick thinking, we* **averted** *an accident.* **Obviate** implies that something, such as a difficulty, has been anticipated and disposed of effectively: *The successful mediation* **obviated** *the need for a lawsuit.* **Forestall** usually suggests anticipatory measures taken to counteract, neutralize, or nullify the effects of something: *We installed an alarm system to* **forestall** *break-ins.*

produce

produce, bear, yield

These verbs mean to bring forth as a product. *The company* **produces** *bottle caps. Trees* **bear** *fruit at different times. The investment* **yielded** *a bonus.*

proficient

proficient, adept, skilled, skillful, expert

These adjectives mean having or showing knowledge, ability, or skill, as in a vocation, profession, or branch of learning. **Proficient** suggests advanced ability gained through training: *It takes many years of study and experience to become a* **proficient** *surgeon.* **Adept** suggests being naturally good at something that one has improved through practice: *The dressmaker became* **adept** *at cutting fabric without a pattern.* **Skilled** suggests sound, thorough ability and often mastery, as in an art, a craft, or a trade: *Only the most* **skilled** *gymnasts are accepted for the Olympic team.* **Skillful** means skilled with a natural knack: *She is especially **skillful** at measuring things by eye.* ***Expert*** applies to one with absolute skill and command: *A virtuoso is one who is **expert** in playing a musical instrument.*

proud proud, arrogant, haughty, disdainful

These adjectives mean filled with or marked by a high opinion of oneself and looking down on what one views as being unworthy. ***Proud*** often means self-satisfied in a conceited way: *They were too **proud** to admit that they needed help.* ***Arrogant*** means overbearingly proud, demanding of more power or consideration than is deserved: *The **arrogant** man refused to stand in line and wait his turn.* ***Haughty*** means proud in a condescending way, as because of one's high birth or station: *The duchess turned away with a **haughty** sniff, ignoring my question.* ***Disdainful*** means proud in a scornful, mocking way: *My teacher is **disdainful** of popular music.*

prudence prudence, discretion, foresight, forethought

These nouns refer to the exercise of good judgment, common sense, and even caution, especially in the conduct of practical matters. ***Prudence*** is the most comprehensive: *The manager's **prudence** when it came to spending money was essential in sticking to the annual budget.* ***Discretion*** suggests wise self-restraint, as in resisting a rash impulse: *As Shakespeare said, "The better part of valor is **discretion**."* ***Foresight*** implies the ability to foresee and make provision for what may happen: *Because we had the **foresight** to check the weather report, we had our umbrellas with us when it started to rain.* ***Forethought*** suggests advance consideration of future eventualities: *The empty refrigerator illustrated a lack of **forethought**.*

pull pull, drag, draw, tow, tug

These verbs mean to apply force to something, causing it to move toward that force. *The children **pulled** their sled up the hill. I had to **drag** my dog away from the cat in the tree. The* *weary traveler* **drew** *his chair closer to the fire. The car was* **towing** *a large trailer. I* **tugged** *my desk to the other side of the room.*

Antonym: push

punish

punish, correct, discipline, penalize

These verbs mean to subject a person to a penalty, such as loss, pain, or confinement, for an offense, a sin, or a fault. ***Punish*** is the most general: *Rather than just* **punish** *bad behavior, you must also reward good behavior.* ***Correct*** means to punish so that the offender will mend his or her ways: *Grandma always* **corrects** *the children when they are rude.* ***Discipline*** stresses punishment by an authority in order to control or correct an offender: *Company policy states that a worker may be* **disciplined** *for carelessness on the job.* ***Penalize*** emphasizes the idea of a penalty: *Anyone who does not hand in the report on time will be* **penalized**.

push

push, propel, shove, thrust

These verbs mean to press against something in order to move it forward or aside. *I* **pushed** *the chair back against the wall. A strong wind* **propelled** *the sailboat. Melissa* **shoved** *her little brother out of the way. He* **thrust** *the stick into the ground.*

Antonym: pull

quality

quality, characteristic, property, attribute, trait

These nouns mean a feature that distinguishes or identifies someone or something. ***Quality*** and ***characteristic*** are the most general: *The voice had a soft, musical* **quality**. *Name a common* **characteristic** *of mammals.* ***Property*** means a basic or essential quality possessed by all members of a group: *This experiment will illustrate some of the* **properties** *of crystals.* ***Attribute*** often means a quality that someone or something is given credit for having: *What are the* **attributes** *of a good leader?* ***Trait*** means a single, clearly defined characteristic: *His jealous streak is a disturbing* **trait**.

quiet

quiet, silent, still

These adjectives mean making little or no noise. *It is best to be* **quiet** *when fishing. The teacher told us to be* **silent** *until everyone finished the test. The audience was* **still** *during the concert.*
Antonym:loud

reach

reach, achieve, attain, gain

These verbs mean to succeed in arriving at a goal or an objective. **Reach** is the most general term: *They* **reached** *shelter just before the storm broke.* **Achieve** suggests reaching by applying one's skill or initiative: *Because of their pioneering research, the team of chemists* **achieved** *international fame.* **Attain** often means to reach because of the force of one's ambitions: *Soon she will* **attain** *her dream of becoming a lawyer.* **Gain** suggests making considerable effort to overcome obstacles: *Slowly the new management* **gained** *our confidence.*

real

real, actual, true

These adjectives mean not imaginary or made up. **Real** suggests that something is genuine or authentic or that it is what it seems to be: *Be careful with the bracelet—it is made of* **real** *gold.* **Actual** means existing and not just potential or possible: *The* **actual** *temperature was sixty degrees, but it seemed colder.* **True** describes something in line with fact, reality, or the actual state of things: *The movie is based on a* **true** *story.*

reason

reason, intuition, understanding, judgment

These nouns refer to the intellectual faculty by which humans seek or attain knowledge or truth. **Reason** is the power to think rationally and logically and to draw inferences: *Through the powers of* **reason**, *the detective was able to deduce who had committed the crime.* **Intuition** is perception or comprehension, as of truths or facts, without the use of the rational process: *I trust my* **intuitions** *when it comes to assessing someone's character.* **Understanding** is the faculty by which one understands, often together with the resulting comprehension: Our **understanding** of deep space is better than what it was fifty years ago. **Judgment** is the ability to assess situations or circumstances and draw sound conclusions: *Benjamin Franklin said, "At twenty years of age, the will reigns; at thirty, the wit; and at forty, the **judgment**."*

recover

recover, regain, retrieve

These verbs mean to get back something lost or taken away. **Recover** is the most general: *The police **recovered** the stolen car.* **Regain** suggests success in recovering something that has been taken from one: *Sabrina **regained** the lead before the race was over.* **Retrieve** refers to the recovery with effort of something: *He **retrieved** the ball from the end zone.*

Antonym: lose

refuse

refuse, decline, reject

These verbs mean to be unwilling to accept, consider, or receive someone or something. **Refuse** can mean to oppose something in an abrupt, rude way: *The captain **refused** to hear of any changes to the plan.* **Decline** means to refuse politely: *He **declined** the job promotion because he wanted to spend more time with his family.* **Reject** suggests casting away someone or something as useless or defective: *The army would **reject** you because of your flat feet.*

Antonym: accept

relieve

relive, allay, alleviate, assuage, mitigate

These verbs mean to make something less severe or more bearable. To **relieve** is to make more endurable something causing discomfort or distress: *Mr. O'Hara took some aspirin to **relieve** his headache.* **Allay** suggests at least temporary relief from what is burdensome or painful: *The workers' fears of being laid off were **allayed** when they were offered a new contract.* **Alleviate** connotes temporary lessening of distress without removal of its cause: *My workload will be **alleviated** when we hire a summer intern.* To **assuage** is to soothe or make milder: *He* *assuaged* his guilt by confessing to the crime. **Mitigate** refers to the moderation of force or intensity: *The architect **mitigated** the impact of the skyscraper on the neighborhood by reducing its height by 150 feet.*

rely

rely, trust, depend

These verbs mean to place or have faith or confidence in someone or something. **Rely** suggests complete confidence: *Presidents must be able to **rely** on their advisers.* **Trust** stresses confidence arising from a belief: *She **trusted** her parents' judgment and did as they suggested.* **Depend** suggests confidence in the help or support of another: *I hope you know you can **depend** on me no matter what happens.*

remember

remember, recall, recollect

These verbs mean to bring an image or a thought back to the mind. *He can't **remember** where he bought the shirt. Once I saw her, I easily **recalled** her name. Can you **recollect** how the accident happened?*

Antonym: forget

revere

revere, worship, adore, idolize

These verbs mean to regard with the deepest respect and honor. **Revere** means to honor and feel awed by something or someone: *Their ancestor is **revered** as one of the town's founders.* **Worship** means to feel reverent or devoted love and often religious faith: *The ancient Greeks **worshiped** many different gods and goddesses.* **Adore** means to worship intensely: *The little girl had such a sweet nature that everyone **adored** her.* **Idolize** means to worship something as if it were perfect: *Karen still **idolizes** her older brother.*

rich

rich, wealthy, affluent

These adjectives mean having a great amount of money, property, or possessions of value. *Rick wants to be **rich** and famous* *someday.* Many **wealthy** *corporations donate money to the arts. The Smiths are the most* **affluent** *family in town.*

Antonym: **poor**

ridicule

ridicule, mock, taunt, deride

These verbs refer to evoking contemptuous laughter about someone. **Ridicule** implies disparaging someone on purpose: *Ted quit the baseball team because the coach kept* **ridiculing** *his attempts to catch the ball.* To **mock** is to poke fun at someone, often by mimicry and caricature: *The comic* **mocked** *the people in the front row by imitating the way they talked.* **Taunt** suggests mocking, insulting, or scornful reproach: *The bully* **taunted** *the younger students on the playground.* **Deride** implies scorn and contempt: *The teacher* **derided** *the students who showed up late to class.*

rip

rip, tear, shred, split

These verbs mean to pull apart or separate by physical effort. **Rip** suggests separation by force, often along a dividing line such as a seam or joint: *The nurses* **ripped** *sheets into long strips to use as bandages.* **Tear** means to pull something apart or into pieces: *He* **tore** *the napkin into bits.* **Shred** means to separate into long, irregular strips: *You should always* **shred** *confidential papers before throwing them away.* **Split** means to cut or break something into parts or layers, especially along its entire length: *They* **split** *the logs with an ax to make firewood.*

rise

rise, ascend, climb, soar

These verbs mean to move upward from a lower to a higher position. **Rise** is the most general: *Fog was* **rising** *from the pond.* **Ascend** frequently suggests a gradual step-by-step rise: *The plane took off and* **ascended** *steadily until it was out of sight.* **Climb** suggests steady progress that often requires some effort, as against gravity: *We* **climbed** *up the steep staircase to the third* *floor.* **Soar** suggests effortless ascending to a great height: *A lone bird* **soared** *into the clouds.*

Antonym: **descend**

rough

rough, harsh, jagged, rugged

These adjectives describe what is not smooth but has a coarse, irregular surface. **Rough** describes something that to the sight or touch has inequalities, as bumps or ridges: *Jane put lotion on her* **rough**, *chapped hands.* **Harsh** means unpleasantly rough, grating, or not harmonious: *The* **harsh** *burlap costume made him itchy.* **Jagged** describes an edge or a surface with ragged, irregular projections and notches: *I almost stepped on that* **jagged** *piece of glass.* **Rugged** describes land surfaces characterized by irregular, often steep rises and slopes: *We had trouble following the* **rugged** *trail.*

Antonym: **smooth**

ruin

ruin, wreck, destroy, demolish

These verbs mean to damage something and deprive it of usefulness, soundness, or value. **Ruin** can mean to harm greatly without necessarily bringing about total destruction: *A flood would* **ruin** *all the books in the basement.* **Wreck** can mean to ruin in or as if in a violent collision: *Six cars were* **wrecked** *when the crane fell in the parking lot.* **Destroy** can mean to damage something so that it is completely obliterated: *The spy* **destroyed** *all evidence of his whereabouts.* **Demolish** means to destroy by pulling down or breaking something to pieces: *The old prison was* **demolished** *to build a new hospital.*

sad

sad, unhappy, melancholy, sorrowful, desolate

These adjectives mean affected with or marked by a lack of joy. **Sad** and **unhappy** are the most general terms: *I was* **sad** *when I heard about that beautiful house being destroyed in the fire. He doesn't like movies that make him* **unhappy**. **Melancholy** means feeling a lingering or habitual sadness: *I kept telling jokes, trying to cheer up our* **melancholy** *dinner compan-*

ion. **Sorrowful** means experiencing a painful sadness, especially one caused by loss: *One of the mourners let out a* ***sorrowful*** *cry.* **Desolate** means sorrowful beyond consolation: *He has been* ***desolate*** *ever since his friend moved away.*

Antonym: glad

satisfy

satisfy, answer, fulfill, meet

These verbs mean to supply fully or completely. *If you* ***satisfy*** *each requirement, then you will pass the class. The city council* ***answered*** *our pleas by repairing the potholes. After years of schooling, Laura* ***fulfilled*** *her aspiration of becoming a dentist. Because the contractor* ***met*** *her obligations a month early, she was paid a bonus.*

save

save, rescue, deliver

These verbs mean to free a person or thing from danger, evil, confinement, or servitude. **Save** is the most general: *The smallpox vaccine has* ***saved*** *many lives.* **Rescue** usually suggests saving from immediate harm or danger by direct action: *All of the passengers and crew were* ***rescued*** *from the sinking ship.* **Deliver** means to liberate people from something such as misery, error, or evil: *Who will* ***deliver*** *them from their enemies?*

scent

scent, aroma, smell, odor

These nouns mean a quality that can be detected by sense organs in the nose. *The* ***scent*** *of pine needles filled the cabin. The* ***aroma*** *of frying onions always makes me hungry. We were alarmed by the* ***smell*** *of gas in the hall. The freshly painted room had a peculiar* ***odor***.

see

see, notice, observe, view

These verbs mean to be visually aware of something. **See** is the most general term: *Did you* ***see*** *the lunar eclipse last night?* **Observe** can mean to look carefully and closely: *We* ***observed*** *a change in the color of the water as it got deeper and deeper.* **Notice** can mean to observe closely and form a rather detailed impression: *He didn't **notice** that frost had formed on the window. **View** can mean to examine with a particular purpose in mind or in a special way: *The jury wished to **view** the evidence again.*

seem

seem, appear, look

These verbs mean to give the impression or idea of being something. *Billy **seems** worried about the test. The assignment **appears** more difficult than it really is. You **look** so happy today.*

send

send, dispatch, forward, transmit

These verbs mean to cause to go or be taken to a destination. *Mom **sent** the package yesterday. They **dispatched** a messenger to the lawyer's office. The post office is **forwarding** their mail to their new address. Be careful not to **transmit** your cold to everyone else.*

separate

separate, divide, part, sever

These verbs mean to cause to become disconnected or disunited. ***Separate** means to put apart or to keep apart: *A mountain range **separates** France and Spain. **Divide** means to separate by cutting, splitting, or branching into parts: *The orange was **divided** into segments. **Part** often means to separate closely associated persons or things: *A difference of opinion **parted** the old friends. **Sever** often means to divide or cut off something abruptly and violently: *The United States **severed** diplomatic relations with Cuba in 1961.*

Antonym: join

shake

shake, tremble, quiver, quake, shiver, shudder

These verbs mean to vibrate involuntarily. ***Shake** is the most general: *The floor **shook** when she jumped up and down. **Tremble** and **quiver** suggest quick, rather slight movement, as from excitement, weakness, or anger: *The frustrated customer **trembled** with rage. His lip **quivers** whenever he is very nervous. **Quake** refers to more violent movement, as that caused by* shock or upheaval: *I was so terrified that my legs began to **quake**. **Shiver** and **shudder** can mean to tremble, especially because of cold, fear or horror: *We noticed someone **shivering** in the snow outside. The stranger's creepy laughter made her **shudder**.*

shelter

shelter, cover, retreat, refuge, asylum, sanctuary

These nouns refer to places that provide protection or to the state of being protected. **Shelter** usually suggests a covered or enclosed area that protects temporarily, as from injury or attack: *We looked for **shelter** from the storm.* **Cover** suggests something, as bushes, that conceals: *They escaped under **cover** of darkness.* **Retreat** refers chiefly to an isolated place to which one retires for meditation, peace, or privacy: *Their cabin in the woods served as a **retreat** from their hectic careers.* **Refuge** suggests a place of escape from pursuit or from difficulties: *Many escaped slaves found **refuge** in Canada.* **Asylum** means a refuge providing legal protection against a pursuer or immunity from arrest: *The political prisoner sought **asylum** in the United States.* **Sanctuary** means a holy or sacred refuge: *They found **sanctuary** in a little church.*

shout

shout, holler, howl, roar, yell

These verbs mean to say with or make a loud, strong cry. *The children **shouted** and ran around the playground. She **hollered** a warning at the trespassers. Kevin dropped the bowling ball on his foot and started **howling** with pain. The audience **roared** with laughter at the clowns. Several people were **yelling** at the umpire.*

show

show, display, expose, parade, exhibit

These verbs mean to present something to view. **Show** is the most general: *Jenny **showed** her classmates the book she was reading.* **Display** often suggests an attempt to present something to best advantage: *The dealer spread the rug out to **display** the pattern.* **Expose** usually involves uncovering something or bringing it out from hiding: *The excavation **exposed*** many Bronze Age artifacts. ***Parade*** usually suggests a flashy or boastful presentation: *The twins came in **parading** their new matching outfits.* ***Exhibit*** suggests open presentation that invites inspection: *The stores **exhibited** their new merchandise in the windows.*

shy

shy, bashful, modest

These adjectives mean not forward but marked by a retiring nature, reticence, or a reserve of manner. ***Shy*** means feeling uneasy around other people, especially strangers, either because of a withdrawn nature or out of fearfulness: *The **shy** new student sat in the back of the classroom.* ***Bashful*** suggests self-consciousness or awkwardness in the presence of others: *Being **bashful**, I didn't laugh too loudly.* ***Modest*** is associated with an unassertive nature, absence of vanity, and freedom from pretension: *Despite her great fame as a gymnast, she remained a **modest** person.*

sign

sign, badge, mark, token

These nouns refer to an outward indication of the existence or presence of something. ***Sign*** is the most general: *You have shown great **signs** of improvement this semester.* ***Badge*** usually refers to something that is worn as an insignia of membership, is an emblem of achievement, or is a characteristic sign: *The sheriff's **badge** was shaped like a star.* ***Mark*** means a sign of a distinctive trait or characteristic: *That question is a **mark** of his intelligence.* ***Token*** usually refers to evidence or proof of something intangible: *Flowers can be a **token** of affection.*

slide

slide, glide, skid, coast

These verbs mean to move smoothly and continuously over or as if over a slippery surface. ***Slide*** suggests rapid, easy movement without loss of contact with the surface: *A tear **slid** down my cheek.* ***Glide*** means to move in a smooth, free-flowing, seemingly effortless way: *A submarine **glided** silently through the water.* ***Skid*** means to slide uncontrollably, often in a sideways direction: *The automobile **skidded** on a patch of ice*. ***Coast*** often means to slide downward, especially when as a result of gravity: *We **coasted** down the hill on our sleds.*

smart

smart, intelligent, bright, brilliant, intellectual

These adjectives mean talented in using one's mind. ***Smart*** means able to learn quickly and often also able to look out for oneself: *Judy was **smart** to tune up her bicycle before the long ride*. ***Intelligent*** means able to handle new situations and problems and good at figuring things out: Only the most ***intelligent*** *students can keep up with the teacher's rapid pace*. ***Bright*** means able to learn quickly and easily: *He is so **bright**, he learned to play chess in one afternoon*. ***Brilliant*** means unusually and impressively intelligent: *The most **brilliant** minds in the country have gathered for this conference*. ***Intellectual*** means able to understand difficult or abstract concepts: *Her **intellectual** abilities help her to understand difficult poetry.*

sparing

sparing, frugal, thrift, economical

These adjectives mean using or showing care with resources, such as money. ***Sparing*** stresses restraint in the use of something: *The quiet soldier was **sparing** of words*. ***Frugal*** implies making sacrifices by doing without from luxuries: *My **frugal** neighbors clip coupons to save money on groceries*. ***Thrifty*** suggests industry, care, and diligence in conserving means: *The **thrifty** treasurer was able to save the group thousands of dollars each year*. ***Economical*** stresses prudence, skillful management, and avoiding waste: *The use of fluorescent bulbs is more **economical** than the use of incandescent ones.*

speak

speak, talk, converse

These verbs mean to express one's thoughts by uttering words. ***Speak*** and ***talk*** are both very general: *The movie star refuses to **speak** to reporters about her private life. I would like to **talk** to you about your book report*. ***Converse*** means to interchange thoughts and ideas by talking: *They spent the evening laughing and **conversing** about old times.*

stay
stay, remain, wait, linger

These verbs mean to continue to be in a given place. ***Stay*** is the most general: *We **stayed** at home all evening.* ***Remain*** often means to continue or to be left after others have gone: *One person should **remain** on watch at night.* ***Wait*** means to stay in readiness, anticipation, or expectation: *I was **waiting** for you in the car.* ***Linger*** means to be slow in leaving: *I **lingered**, enjoying the starry night after the fireworks had ended.*

stiff
stiff, rigid, inflexible, inelastic

These adjectives describe what is very firm and does not easily bend or give way. ***Stiff***, the least specific, refers to what can be bent only with difficulty: *My hairbrush has **stiff** bristles.* ***Rigid*** and ***inflexible*** apply to what cannot be bent without damage or deformation: *The container was made of **rigid** plastic. My jackknife has an **inflexible** knife blade.* ***Inelastic*** refers to what will not stretch and spring back without marked physical change: *The spring was useless because it had been pulled too far and had become **inelastic**.*

stop
stop, cease, halt, quit

These verbs mean to bring or come to an end. ***Stop*** *making so much noise while I'm trying to sleep! The siren **ceased** abruptly. We were **halted** at the checkpoint on the border. They **quit** riding at sundown.*

Antonym: start

strange
strange, peculiar, odd, singular, eccentric, curious

These adjectives describe what varies from the usual or customary. ***Strange*** refers especially to what is unfamiliar, unknown, or inexplicable: *I had a very **strange** dream last night.* ***Peculiar*** particularly describes what is distinct from all others: *That kitchen cleanser has a **peculiar** odor.* ***Odd*** describes something that fails to accord with what is ordinary, usual, or expected: *I find it **odd** that her name is never mentioned.* **Singular** describes what is unique or unparalleled and often suggests an unusual or peculiar quality that inspires curiosity or wonder: *Such insight is **singular** in one so young.* **Eccentric** refers particularly to what differs strikingly from the recognized or conventional: *He was considered a brilliant but **eccentric** artist.* **Curious** suggests strangeness or novelty that excites interest: *The platypus is a **curious** animal.*

strength

strength, power, might, force

These nouns mean the capacity to act or work effectively. **Strength** means great physical, mental, or moral energy: *Jennifer gathered her **strength** and moved the boulder out of the way.* **Power** means the ability to do something and especially to produce an effect: *Only the king had the **power** to call the legislature together.* **Might** often means great power: *We would devote all our **might** to a just cause.* **Force** often means the application of strength or power: *He used great **force** in moving the furniture.*

subject

subject, matter, topic, theme

These nouns mean the principal idea or point of a speech, a piece of writing, or a work of art. **Subject** is the most general: *Many eighteenth-century paintings have historical **subjects**.* **Matter** often means the material that is the object of thought: *This will be an interesting **matter** for you to discuss.* **Topic** means a subject of discussion, argument, or conversation: *The hospital is giving a series of lectures on the **topic** of nutrition.* **Theme** often means a subject, idea, point of view, or perception that is developed in a work of art: *The **theme** of this poem is the healing power of love.*

suggest

suggest, imply, hint

These verbs mean to show thoughts or ideas indirectly. **Suggest** is the most general: *Katie's attitude **suggests** she is angry,* *but she hasn't said anything.* **Imply** means to suggest a thought or an idea that is not expressed but that can be figured out from something else: *I didn't mean to **imply** that the situation is hopeless.* **Hint** refers to a roundabout suggestion that often contains clues: *He **hinted** that he would come if he were invited.*

surprise   surprise, astonish, amaze, astound

These verbs mean to affect a person strongly as being unexpected or unusual. **Surprise** means to fill with often sudden wonder or disbelief: *It **surprises** me that you would want a job like that.* **Astonish** means to overwhelm with surprise: *The sight of such an enormous crowd outside the house **astonished** them.* **Amaze** means to affect with great wonder: *The daredevil's feats have **amazed** audiences around the world.* **Astound** means to shock with surprise: *They were **astounded** by the waiter's rudeness.*

suspend   suspend, defer, postpone, shelve

These verbs mean to put off until a later time. *We **suspended** making a judgment until we knew all the facts. The club **deferred** that discussion until the next meeting. Sarah had to **postpone** her trip to Alaska. We could not reach an agreement, so we **shelved** the issue.*

tall   tall, high, lofty, towering, elevated

These adjectives mean extending to a greater than usual height. **Tall** often describes a living thing or something that has great height in relation to width or in comparison with like things: *Abraham Lincoln was a **tall**, lanky man.* **High** refers to what rises a considerable distance from a base or is situated at a level well above another level considered as a base: *The apartment had unusually **high** ceilings.* **Lofty** describes what is of imposing or inspiring height: *We looked up at the **lofty** mountains.* **Towering** suggests awe-inspiring height: *That **towering** oak tree may be a hundred years old.* **Ele-**

vated stresses height in relation to immediate surroundings. It refers especially to being raised or situated above a normal or average level: *The speaker stood on an **elevated** platform.*

Antonyms: **low, short**

tardy

tardy, behindhand, late, overdue

These adjectives mean not arriving, occurring, acting, or done at the scheduled, expected, or usual time: *Michael was **tardy** for class and had to write an essay explaining why he wasn't on time. If you get **behindhand** with your car payments, your car could be repossessed. Anne was **late** for the plane, so she had to take a different flight. Larry had to pay a fine when he returned his **overdue** library books.*

task

task, job, chore, assignment

These nouns mean a piece of work that one must do. ***Task*** means a well-defined responsibility that is sometimes burdensome and is usually required by someone else: *The receptionist's main **task** is to answer the telephones.* ***Job*** often means a specific short-term piece of work: *We spent the day doing odd **jobs** around the house.* ***Chore*** often means a minor, routine, or odd job: *I finished my **chores** before supper.* ***Assignment*** usually means a task given to one by a person in authority: *For tonight's **assignment**, read the first chapter.*

taste

taste, flavor, savor, tang

These nouns mean a quality that can be sensed by the mouth. *Sardines have a salty **taste**. They prefer foods with a spicy **flavor**. The **savor** of freshly brewed coffee always perks me up. The fresh **tang** of lemonade is perfect on a hot day.*

teach

teach, train, instruct, educate, school

These verbs mean to pass on knowledge or skill. ***Teach*** is the most general: *Your sister can **teach** you how to ride a bicycle.* ***Train*** means to teach particular skills intended to fit a person for a certain role, such as a job: *It is the manager's responsibility* to **train** every new employee. **Instruct** usually means to teach in an organized way: *The manual **instructs** you how to assemble the stereo.* **Educate** often means to instruct in a formal way: *Their children were **educated** in the best schools.* **School** often means to teach with a demanding process: *The violinist was **schooled** to practice slowly.*

thoughtful

thoughtful, considerate, attentive, solicitous

These adjectives mean having or showing concern for the well-being of others. ***Thoughtful*** implies a tendency to think of another person's needs or wishes in advance: *It was **thoughtful** of you to bring pretzels to my party.* **Considerate** stresses sensitivity to another's feelings: *To be **considerate** to his parents, John turned the volume down on his radio after they went to bed.* **Attentive** suggests devoted, thorough attention: *An editor who is **attentive** to detail will catch numerous errors.* **Solicitous** implies deep, almost anxious concern that is often expressed with exaggerated attentiveness: *My **solicitous** and meddlesome cousin is always offering advice when it is not asked for.*

throw

throw, hurl, fling, pitch, toss

These verbs mean to shoot something through the air with a motion of the hand or arm. ***Throw*** is the most general: *Toby **threw** a life preserver to the struggling swimmer.* **Hurl** and ***fling*** mean to throw with great force: *In Greek mythology Zeus **hurls** lightning bolts from Olympus as if they were spears. The paper carrier had **flung** the newspaper onto the porch.* **Pitch** often means to throw with careful aim: *She **pitched** the paper into the wastebasket.* **Toss** usually means to throw lightly or casually: *He **tossed** his key onto the desk.*

tire

tire, weary, fatigue, exhaust

These verbs mean to drain of strength, energy, spirit, interest, or patience. ***Tire***, the most general, often describes a state resulting from exertion, excess, dullness, or boredom: *Long* *hours of difficult hiking **tire** the scouts.* **Weary** often suggests dissatisfaction or boredom more strongly: *We soon **wearied** of their constant bickering.* **Fatigue** describes great weariness, as that caused by stress: *All week she has seemed ill and easily **fatigued.*** **Exhaust** means to wear out completely. The term suggests total draining of physical or emotional strength: *By the time I had finished chopping the wood, I was **exhausted.***

turn

turn, rotate, spin, whirl, swirl

These verbs mean to move or cause to move in a circle. **Turn** is the most general: *The boy in front of me **turned** and stared at my desk.* **Rotate** means to move around an axis or center: *The top **rotated** with decreasing speed as the spring wound down.* **Spin** means to rotate rapidly, often within a narrow space: *The sheets were **spinning** in the dryer.* **Whirl** means to rotate or turn rapidly or forcefully: *They saw the **whirling** snowflakes and knew the blizzard had started.* **Swirl** often means to move rapidly in a circle: *Flood waters **swirled** wildly under the bridge.*

uncertainty

uncertainty, doubt, suspicion, mistrust

These nouns mean a condition of being unsure about someone or something. **Uncertainty** is the least forceful: *I looked back on my decision with growing **uncertainty.*** **Doubt** refers to a questioning state of mind that leads to hesitation in accepting something or making a decision: *If there is any **doubt** about his story, you can call his office to confirm it.* **Suspicion** often suggests an uneasy feeling that something or someone is evil: *The leaders from the warring countries regarded each other with **suspicion** at the start of the conference.* **Mistrust** means a lack of trust or confidence arising from suspicion: *After the strike, the company was filled with an atmosphere of general **mistrust.***

unruly

unruly, intractable, recalcitrant, headstrong

These adjectives mean resistant to control. **Unruly** indicates a failure to submit to rule or discipline: *The student was punished* for **unruly** behavior in class. **Intractable** refers to what is obstinate and difficult to manage or control: *The social worker found a loving foster family for the* **intractable** *runaway*. A person who is **recalcitrant** rebels against authority: *The police arrested the* **recalcitrant** *demonstrators*. **Headstrong** describes one obstinately bent on having his or her own way: *The* **headstrong** *senator ignored his constituency*.

uproar   uproar, din, racket, noise

These nouns refer to loud, confused, or disagreeable sound or sounds. **Uproar** means disorder with loud, bewildering sound: *Even indoors we could hear the* **uproar** *of the crowd cheering during the parade*. **Din** means a jumble of loud sounds that usually clash: *The* **din** *in the factory ends abruptly when the noon whistle sounds*. **Racket** means loud, distressing noise: *The toddlers were making a* **racket** *clanging pots and pans together*. **Noise** is the most general term: *Earplugs cannot completely protect your hearing from damage due to* **noise***.*

use   use, employ, utilize

These verbs mean to bring or put someone or something into service in order to make him, her, or it useful, functional, or helpful. **Use** and **employ** mean to put into service or apply for a purpose: *Try* **using** *a stick to stir the paint*. *She* **employed** *her knowledge of Spanish and French on the trip*. **Utilize** especially means to make something profitable or to find new and practical uses for something: *Solar energy can be* **utilized** *to generate electricity*.

vague   vague, ambiguous, obscure, cryptic

These adjectives mean lacking a clear meaning. **Vague** means unclear because of a lack of clarity or precision in expression or thought: *I have only a* **vague** *idea of what the book is about*. **Ambiguous** means having two or more possible meanings: *Frustrated by* **ambiguous** *instructions, the parents were never able to assemble the swing set*. **Obscure** suggests a hidden meaning: *The document makes several **obscure** references to a hidden treasure.* ***Cryptic*** suggests something that is overly brief and that is meant to be puzzling: *The club used **cryptic** abbreviations for everything in order to maintain complete secrecy.*

Antonym: clear

valid

valid, sound, cogent, convincing

These adjectives describe statements, arguments, conclusions, reasons, or intellectual processes that are persuasive because they are well founded. What is ***valid*** is based on or borne out by truth or fact or has legal force: *If you're absent from school, you'll need a **valid** excuse.* What is ***sound*** is free from logical flaws or is based on valid reasoning: *Their hypothesis was based on **sound** principles.* Something ***cogent*** is both sound and compelling: *The witness provided **cogent** testimony at the trial.* ***Convincing*** implies the power to dispel doubt or overcome resistance or opposition: *The lawyer had **convincing** proof of the plaintiff's guilt.*

vertical

vertical, upright, perpendicular

These adjectives mean being at or approximately at right angles to the horizon or to level ground. ***Vertical*** and especially ***upright*** are often used to compare with what is horizontal. The terms do not always describe an exact right angle: *They chose a wallpaper with **vertical** stripes. Amazingly, the tree remained **upright** after the storm.* ***Perpendicular*** generally refers to an angle of exactly ninety degrees: *The table legs were **perpendicular** to the ground.*

Antonym: horizontal

victory

victory, conquest, triumph

These nouns refer to the fact of winning or the state of having won in a war, struggle, or competition. ***Victory***, the most general term, refers especially to the final defeat of an enemy or opponent: *One home run meant all the difference between **victory** and defeat.* ***Conquest*** suggests subduing, subjugating, or achieving mastery or control over someone or something: *It's a science fiction story about the **conquest** of Earth by Martians.* **Triumph** means a victory or success that is especially noteworthy because it is decisive or spectacular: *The play's opening night was a **triumph** for the actors.*

vigor

vigor, punch, verve, vim, vitality

These nouns denote a quality of spirited force or energy: *The **vigor** of the tennis players made the match exciting to watch. The professor wrote an essay with real **punch**. The passionate artist painted with **verve**. My older brother argued with his usual **vim**. The **vitality** of the volunteers made the fundraiser a success.*

vow

vow, promise, pledge, swear

These verbs mean to declare solemnly that one will perform or avoid a particular course of action. *The protesters **vowed** they would never give up their cause. I **promise** to write back soon. Various countries **pledged** to obey the ban on whale hunting. In those movies, the villain always **swears** he will seek revenge.*

wander

wander, ramble, roam, meander

These verbs mean to move about at random or without destination or purpose. ***Wander*** and ***ramble*** both mean to move about without a fixed course or goal: *He **wandered** from room to room looking for something interesting to do. After breakfast we can **ramble** through the hills.* **Roam** suggests wandering with freedom of movement, especially over a wide area: *Herds of bison once **roamed** across the Great Plains.* **Meander** suggests wandering leisurely and sometimes aimlessly over an irregular or winding course: *Susie is **meandering** down to the beach at her own pace.*

way

way, route, course, passage, pass

These nouns refer to paths leading from one place or point to another. ***Way*** is the most general: *Show me the **way** to the* *movie theater.* **Route** refers to a planned, well-established, or regularly traveled way: *There are thirty houses on my paper* **route**. **Course** suggests the path or channel taken by something moving, such as a river or a satellite: *Part of the state line follows the* **course** *of a river.* **Passage** means a connecting way over, across, or through something: *The* **passage** *between the buildings is dark and cramped.* **Pass** usually refers to a passage around, over, or through a barrier: *The* **pass** *between the mountains was so narrow we could get through only one at a time.*

weak

weak, feeble, frail, fragile

These adjectives mean lacking or showing a lack of strength. **Weak**, the most general, suggests lack of physical, mental, or spiritual strength or deficiency of will or purpose: *You feel* **weak** *because you haven't eaten anything all day.* **Feeble** suggests pathetic or serious physical or mental weakness or hopeless inadequacy: *The troublemakers made a* **feeble** *effort to defend their actions.* **Frail** suggests delicacy, as of constitution, or lack of ability to endure or withstand: *She was* **frail** *as a child, but regular exercise helped her grow stronger.* **Fragile** means easily broken, damaged, or destroyed: *His mood was very* **fragile**.

Antonym: strong

wet

wet, moist, damp, humid

These adjectives mean covered with or filled with liquid. **Wet** is the most general: *Marcia hung the* **wet** *towels on the clothesline.* **Moist** means slightly wet: *He wiped off the table with a* **moist** *sponge.* **Damp** means moist and often also unpleasantly sticky: *The* **damp** *cellar had a moldy smell.* **Humid** refers to a disagreeably high degree of water vapor in the atmosphere: *The hot,* **humid** *weather made us want to jump in the pond.*

Antonym: dry

wonder

wonder, marvel, miracle, sensation

These nouns mean something that causes amazement or admiration in others. *If you want to see* **wonders** *of*

architecture, go see the Egyptian pyramids. That dinner was
no **marvel**. The artificial heart is a **miracle** of medical science.
Her most recent book, which has already won three literary
prizes, is a **sensation**.

work

work, labor, toil, drudgery

These nouns refer to physical or mental effort expended to
produce or accomplish something. **Work**, the most general,
can refer both to the activity and the output of persons, of
machines, and of the forces of nature: *Most of the **work** is
already finished.* **Labor** usually suggests human work, especially of a hard physical or intellectual nature: *It took months
of **labor** to dig the tunnel.* **Toil** refers mostly to intense,
fatiguing labor: *The harvesters did not look forward to a long
day of **toil** in the hot sun.* **Drudgery** suggests dull, wearisome,
or monotonous work: *Nothing could ease the **drudgery** of
that awful job.*

yield

yield, abandon, surrender, cede, waive

These verbs mean to let something go or to give something
up. **Yield** suggests giving way, such as to pressure or superior
authority: *The diplomat had **yielded** a lot of ground by the time
the conversation with the President was finished.* **Abandon**
means to let something go or give something up with no
expectation of returning to it or recovering it: *The ship-
wrecked family slowly **abandoned** all hope of being rescued.*
Surrender means to abandon under force or demand: *The
passengers **surrendered** their luggage to the customs agents.* **Cede**
suggests giving up something by formal transfer: *Germany
ceded the region to France as part of the peace treaty.* **Waive**
means voluntarily to do away with something, such as a
claim: *The club members **waived** several of their privileges.*

young

young, youthful, immature, juvenile, green

These adjectives mean of, relating to, characteristic of, or
being in an early period of growth or development. **Young**

is the most general: *You're too **young** to remember life before television.* **Youthful** suggests characteristics, such as enthusiasm, freshness, or energy, that are associated with youth: *My grandfather still has a **youthful** attitude toward life.* **Immature** describes what is not yet fully grown or developed. The term sometimes suggests that someone falls short of an expected level of maturity: *The **immature** brat threw a tantrum in the middle of the store.* **Juvenile** suggests immaturity, often childishness: *They spent April Fools' Day playing **juvenile** pranks.* **Green** suggests lack of training or experience and sometimes callowness: *Those **green** recruits weren't sure how to deal with the emergency.*

Antonyms: mature, old

zest

zest, gusto, relish

These nouns mean intense, hearty pleasure or appreciation. *The **zest** that the volunteers brought to the project made the hard work seem like fun. She tells those old jokes with great **gusto**. He read horror stories with a **relish** that I found disturbing.*

Index to the Thesaurus

This alphabetical index shows you where you can find synonyms and antonyms in your thesaurus. For example, the index entry

enormous see *large*

indicates that to find synonyms for the word *enormous*, you must look under the entry for *large*. There you will find other synonyms, in this case *big*, *great*, and *huge*.

Headwords of entries are listed in color by themselves in the same index. For example, the index entry

rely

shows that *rely* is an entry in the thesaurus at which you will find synonyms for *rely*.

If a headword of an entry also appears at another entry as a synonym, the index entry will be repeated. For example, the index entries

bright

bright *see also* smart

indicate that *bright* is an entry in the thesaurus and the word *bright* also appears at the entry for *smart*.

Some words appear as synonyms in more than one entry. If the words are the same part of speech, the word will be listed once with a comma separating the entries where you will find the word. For example, the index entry

split *see* break, rip

indicates that the word *split* appears at the entries for both *break* and *rip*.

Words that appear more than once in the synonym lists as different parts of speech will be repeated in the index with the part of speech given in parentheses next to the entry. For example, the index entries

relish (*verb*) *see* love

relish (*noun*) *see* zest

indicate that *relish* appears at two places, once as a verb and once as a noun.

Antonyms are marked by the phrase *see antonym at*. For example, the index entry

add *see antonym at* decrease

indicates that to find *decrease* used as an antonym, you must look under the entry for *add*, where you will find *decrease*.

Index

abandon *see* yield
ability
absurd *see* foolish
abuse *see antonym at* pamper
accept *see antonym at* refuse
acclaim *see* praise
accommodate *see* adapt, contain
accompany
accomplish *see* perform
accumulate *see* gather
achieve *see* perform, reach
acknowledge
active
actual *see* real
adapt
add *see antonym at* decrease
adept *see* proficient
adjust *see* adapt
admit *see* acknowledge
adore *see* revere
adroit *see* dexterous
advantageous *see* beneficial
adventuresome *see* adventurous
adventurous
affect
affluent *see* rich
agree
aid *see* help
aim
aim *see also* intention
alarm *see* frighten
alert *see* aware
allay *see* relieve
alleviate *see* relieve

allow *see antonym at* forbid
alone
also *see* besides
alternative *see* choice
amaze *see* surprise
ambiguous *see* vague
amuse
ancient *see* old
anger
annoy
answer
answer *see antonym at* ask
answer *see also* satisfy
anticipate *see* expect
antique *see* old
anxiety
apparent *see* clear
appear *see* seem
appease *see* pacify
appreciate
apprehend
approve
aptitude *see* ability
arbiter *see* judge
arbitrator *see* judge
arcane *see* mysterious
argue
aroma *see* scent
arrogant *see* proud
ascend *see* rise
ask
ask *see antonym at* answer
assemble *see* gather
assignment *see* task
assist *see* help
assuage *see* relieve
astonish *see* surprise
astound *see* surprise

asylum *see* shelter
athletic *see* muscular
attain *see* reach
attentive *see* thoughtful
attribute *see* quality
auspicious *see* favorable
authentic
average
avert *see* prevent
await *see* expect
aware

baby *see* pamper
bad
badge *see* sign
bailiwick *see* field
ban *see* forbid
banish
bare *see* empty
bashful *see* shy
bear *see* produce
beat *see* defeat
beautiful
begin
begin *see antonym at* complete
behindhand *see* tardy
bend
beneficial
besides
bicker *see* argue
big *see* large
big *see antonym at* little
blank *see* empty
blend *(verb) see* mix
blend *(noun) see* mixture
blubber *see* cry
blue *see* depressed
boast
bold *see* brave
boost *see* lift

Index

border *see* margin
boring
bother *see* annoy
brag *see* boast
brave
brawny *see* muscular
breach
break
bright
bright *see also* smart
brilliant *see* bright,
   smart
brink *see* margin
burly *see* muscular
burn
bury *see* hide
business

calculate
calm
cancel *see* erase
candid *see* frank
care
care *see also* anxiety
careful
careless *see antonym at*
   careful
case *see* example
catch
cease *see* stop
ceaseless *see* continual
cede *see* yield
celebrated *see* noted
center
certify *see* approve
chance *see* happen
chaperone *see*
   accompany
char *see* burn
characteristic *see*
   quality

charge *see* care
cheap *see antonym at*
   expensive
cheerful *see* glad
cherish *see* appreciate
chief
chilly *see* cold
choice
chore *see* task
chubby *see* fat
circumstance *see*
   occurrence
civil *see* polite
clean
clean *see antonym at*
   dirty
cleanly *see* clean
clear
clear *see antonym at*
   vague
climb *see* rise
close *see* complete
coast *see* slide
coddle *see* pamper
cogent *see* valid
coincide *see* agree
cold
collect *see* gather
combat *see* conflict
combat *see* oppose
combine *see* join
comfortable
comical *see* funny
commence *see* begin
commend *see* praise
comment
commerce *see* business
common
compassion *see* pity
complete
complex

complicated *see* complex
composite *see* mixture
compound *see* mixture
comprehend *see*
   apprehend
compute *see* calculate
conceal *see* hide
concept *see* idea
concern *see* anxiety
conclude *see* complete,
   decide
condone *see* forgive
conducive *see* favorable
conduct *see* accompany
confess *see* acknowledge
conflict
conform *see* adapt, agree
connect *see* join
conquer *see* defeat
conquest *see* victory
conscious *see* aware
consequence *see* effect,
   importance
considerate *see*
   thoughtful
constant *see* continual
consume *see* eat
contain
contest *(noun) see*
   conflict
contest *(verb) see*
   oppose
continual
continuous *see*
   continual
contour *see* outline
converse *see* speak
convincing *see* valid
cooperative *see antonym*
   at obstinate
copy *see* imitate

Index

correct *see* punish
correspond *see* agree
costly *see* expensive
courageous *see* brave
course *see* way
courteous *see* polite
cover *see* shelter
cowardly *see antonym at* brave
cozy *see* comfortable
crack *see* break
crave *see* desire
create *see* establish
crow *see* boast
cruel
crush
cry
cryptic *see* vague
curious
curious *see also* strange
curve *see* bend
custom *see* habit

damage *see* hurt
damp *see* wet
daredevil *see* adventurous
daring *see* adventurous
dark
dark *see antonym at* bright
deal *see* distribute
deceive
decide
decline *see* refuse
decrease
decrease *see antonym at* increase
defeat
defend

defer *see* suspend
deft *see* dexterous
dejected *see* depressed
delete *see* erase
deliver *see* save
delude *see* deceive
demolish *see* ruin
depend *see* rely
deport *see* banish
depressed
deride *see* ridicule
descend *see antonym at* rise
describe
design *see* plan
desire
desolate *see* sad
destroy *see* ruin
devour *see* eat
dexterous
difficult *see antonym at* easy
dim *see* dark
diminish *see* decrease
din *see* uproar
direct *see* aim
dirty
dirty *see antonym at* clean
disagree *see antonym at* agree
disappear
discipline *see* punish
discretion *see* prudence
disdainful *see* proud
dislike *see antonym at* love
dispatch *see* send
dispense *see* distribute
display *see* show
distribute
divide *see* distribute,

separate
divide *see antonym at* join
domain *see* field
doubt *see* uncertainty
downcast *see* depressed
downhearted *see* depressed
drag *see* pull
draw *see* pull
dread *see* fear
drudgery *see* work
dry *see antonym at* wet
dull *see* boring
dull *see antonym at* interesting
dupe *see* deceive
dusky *see* dark
duty *see* obligation
dwindle *see* decrease
dynamic *see* active

easy
eat
eccentric *see* strange
economical *see* sparing
edge *see* margin
educate *see* teach
effect
effortless *see* easy
elevated *see* tall
elucidate *see* explain
embark *see* begin
emotion *see* feeling
employ *see* use
empty
end *see* complete, intention
end *see antonym at* begin
endanger

Index

endorse *see* approve
energetic *see* active
engaging *see* interesting
enjoy *see* love
enlarge *see* increase
enormous *see* large
ensue *see* follow
entertain *see* amuse
erase
escort *see* accompany
esoteric *see* mysterious
establish
evaporate *see* disappear
even *see* flat
event *see* occurrence
evil *see* bad
examine *see* ask
example
example *see also* ideal
excuse *see* forgive
execute *see* perform
exhaust *see* tire
exhibit *see* show
exile *see* banish
expand *see* increase
expect
expensive
expert *see* proficient
explain
expose *see* show
expound *see* explain
expunge *see* erase
extend *see* increase
extol *see* praise
extradite *see* banish

fade *see* disappear
fair
fair *see also* average
faithful
familiar *see* common
famous *see* noted

fancy *see* love
fascinating *see*
   interesting
fashion
fast
fat
fat *see antonym at* lean
fatigue *see* tire
faultless *see* perfect
favorable
fear
fearless *see* brave
feeble *see* weak
feeling
ferocious *see* cruel
fertile
field
fierce *see* cruel
fight *(noun) see* conflict
fight *(verb) see* oppose
filthy *see* dirty
final *see* last
firm
first *see antonym at* last
flash *see* moment
flat
flavor *see* taste
flawless *see* perfect
flexible *see antonym at*
   obstinate
fling *see* throw
focus *see* center
follow
foolish
forbid
force *see* strength
foresight *see* prudence
forestall *see* prevent
forethought *see*
   prudence
forget *see antonym at*
   remember

forgive
forward *see* send
foul *see* dirty
found *see* establish
fragile *see* weak
frail *see* weak
frank
fresh *see* new
fright *see* fear
frighten
frigid *see* cold
frosty *see* cold
frugal *see* sparing
fruitful *see* fertile
fulfill *see* perform,
   satisfy
full *see antonym at*
   empty
funny
furthermore *see* besides
fury *see* anger
fuse *see* mix

gag *see* joke
gain *see* reach
gather
gather *see antonym at*
   distribute
gaze *see* look
genuine *see* authentic
glad
glad *see antonym at* sad
glide *see* slide
goal *see* intention
good *see antonym*
   at bad
grand *see* magnificent
grandiose *see*
   magnificent
grasp *see* apprehend
great *see* large
green *see* young

Index

grimy *see* dirty
guard *see* defend
guide
guileless *see* naive
gusto *see* zest

habit
halt *see* stop
handy *see* dexterous
happen
happy *see* glad
harass
hard *see* firm
hardy *see* healthy
harry *see* harrass
harsh *see* rough
haste *see* hurry
hasty *see* fast
hate *see antonym at* love
haughty *see* proud
headquarters *see* center
headstrong *see*
    obstinate, unruly
heal *see antonym at*
    hurt
healthy
heap
heave *see* lift
heavy
hefty *see* heavy
help
help *see antonym at* hurt
hide
high *see* tall
hint *see* suggest
hoist *see* lift
hold *see* contain
holler *see* shout
hope *see* expect
horizontal *see antonym*
    at vertical
horror *see* fear

hot *see antonym at* cold
hound *see* harrass
howl *see* shout
hub *see* center
huge *see* large
humid *see* wet
humor *see* mood
humorous *see* funny
hurl *see* throw
hurry
hurt

icy *see* cold
idea
ideal
idolize *see* revere
illustration *see* example
illustrious *see* noted
imitate
immaculate *see* clean
immature *see* young
impeccable *see* perfect
imperil *see* endanger
imply *see* suggest
importance
imposing *see*
    magnificent
improve *see antonym at*
    hurt
incident *see* occurrence
increase
indifferent *see antonym*
    at curious
indignation *see* anger
indulge *see* pamper
industry *see* business
inelastic *see* stiff
inflexible *see* stiff
influence *see* affect
information *see*
    knowledge
infraction *see* breach

infringement *see*
    breach
injure *see* hurt
inquire *see* ask
inquisitive *see* curious
instant *see* moment
institute *see* establish
instruct *see* teach
insult *see* offend
intellectual *see* smart
intelligent *see* smart
intent *see* intention
intention
interesting
interesting *see antonym*
    at boring
interfere
intermission *see* pause
interpret *see* explain
intractable *see* unruly
intricate *see* complex
intriguing *see*
    interesting
intuition *see* reason
involved *see* complex
irritate *see* annoy

jagged *see* rough
jeopardize *see* endanger
jerk
jest *see* joke
jiffy *see* moment
job *see* task
join
join *see antonym at*
    separate
joke
joyful *see* glad
judge
judgment *see* reason
just *see* fair
juvenile *see* young

Index

keep
keeping *see* care
knotty *see* complex
knowledge

label *see* mark
labor *see* work
large
last
late *see* tardy
laugh *see antonym at* cry
laughable *see* funny
lead *see* guide
lean
lean *see antonym at* fat
learning *see* knowledge
lessen *see* decrease
level *(verb) see* aim
level *(adjective) see* flat
lift
light *see antonyms at* dark, heavy
lighthearted *see* glad
like *see* love
likewise *see* besides
linger *see* stay
link *see* join
little
lively *see* active
lively *see antonym at* boring
lofty *see* tall
lonely *see* alone
lonesome *see* alone
look
look *see also* seem
lose *see antonym at* recover
loud *see antonym at* quiet
love
lovely *see* beautiful

low *see antonym at* tall
loyal *see* faithful
luminous *see* bright

magnificent
main *see* chief
majestic *see* magnificent
manner *see* method
mannerly *see* polite
margin
marine *see* nautical
maritime *see* nautical
mark *(verb)*
mark *(noun) see* sign
marvel *see* wonder
mash *see* crush
massive *see* heavy
matter *see* subject
mature *see antonym at* young
meander *see* wander
meddle *see* interfere
mediocre *see* average
medium *see* average
meet *see* satisfy
melancholy *see* sad
merge *see* mix
messy *see antonym at* neat
method
might *see* strength
mimic *see* imitate
mindful *see* careful
mingle *see* mix
miniature *see* little
miracle *see* wonder
mislead *see* deceive
mistrust *see* uncertainty
mitigate *see* relieve
mix
mixture
mock *see* ridicule

mode *see* fashion
model *see* ideal
modern *see antonym at* old
modest *see* shy
moist *see* wet
mollify *see* pacify
moment
mood
mound *see* heap
move *see* affect
mulish *see* obstinate
multiply *see* increase
murky *see* dark
muscular
mysterious

naive
narrate *see* describe
nautical
naval *see* nautical
neat
new
newfangled *see* new
nimble *see* dexterous
noise *see* uproar
normal
nosy *see* curious
noted
notice *see* see
notion *see* idea
novel *see* new

object *see* intention
objective *see* fair
obligation
obscure *see* dark, vague
obscure *see antonym at* noted
observant *see* careful
observation *see* comment
observe *see* see

Index

obsolete *see* old
obstinate
obviate *see* prevent
obvious *see* clear
occult *see* mysterious
occur *see* happen
occurrence
odd *see* strange
odor *see* scent
offend
old
old *see antonyms at* new,
  young
oppose
option *see* choice
ordinary *see* common
origin
original *see* new
outcome *see* effect
outline
outrage *see* offend
outspoken *see* frank
overdue *see* tardy

pacify
pamper
panic *see* frighten
parade *see* show
parch *see* burn
pardon *see* forgive
part *see* separate
pass *see* way
passage *see* way
passion *see* feeling
pause
peaceful *see* calm
peculiar *see* strange
penalize *see* punish
perfect
perform
perpendicular *see*
  vertical

perpetual *see* continual
pester *see* harrass
pile *see* heap
pitch *see* throw
pity
placate *see* pacify
placid *see* calm
plain *see* clear
plan
pledge *see* vow
plump *see* fat
point *see* aim
polite
poor *see antonym at* rich
postpone *see* suspend
power *see* strength
practice *see* habit
praise
preclude *see* prevent
preference *see* choice
preserve *see* defend
pretty *see* beautiful
prevent
priceless *see* expensive
primary *see* chief
principal *see* chief
prize *see* appreciate
produce
productive *see* fertile
proficient
profile *see* outline
profitable *see* beneficial
prohibit *see* forbid
project *see* plan
prolific *see* fertile
promise *see* vow
propel *see* push
property *see* quality
propitious *see* favorable
protect *see* defend
proud
province *see* field

provoke *see* annoy
prudence
pudgy *see* fat
pull
pull *see antonym at* push
pulp *see* crush
punch *see* vigor
punish
punish *see antonym at*
  pamper
purpose *see* intention
push
push *see antonym at*
  pull

quake *see* shake
quality
quarrel *see* argue
question *see* ask
quick *see* fast
quiet
quit *see* stop
quiver *see* shake
quiz *see* ask

racket *see* uproar
radiant *see* bright
rage *see* anger
raise *see* lift
ramble *see* wander
rapid *see* fast
ratify *see* approve
ration *see* distribute
reach
real
real *see also* authentic
realm *see* field
reason
recalcitrant *see* unruly
recall *see* remember
recess *see* pause
reckon *see* calculate

Index

recollect *see* remember
recover
reduce *see* decrease
referee *see* judge
refuge *see* shelter
refuse
regain *see* recover
regale *see* amuse
regular *see* normal
reject *see* refuse
relate *see* describe
relieve
relish *(noun) see* zest
relish *(verb) see* love
rely
remain *see* stay
remark *see* comment
remember
renowned *see* noted
reply *see* answer
report *see* describe
rescue *see* save
reserve *see* keep
resist *see* oppose
resolve *see* decide
respond *see* answer
responsibility *see*
obligation
restful *see* comfortable
result *(noun) see* effect
result *(verb) see* follow
retain *see* keep
retort *see* answer
retreat *see* shelter
retrieve *see* recover
revere
rich
ridicule
ridiculous *see* foolish
rigid *see* stiff
rim *see* margin
rip

rise
risk *see* endanger
roam *see* wander
roar *see* shout
robust *see* healthy
root *see* origin
rotate *see* turn
rough
round *see* bend
route *see* way
routine *see* method
rude *see antonym at*
polite
rugged *see* rough
ruin
rule *see* decide

sad
sad *see antonym at*
glad
sample *see* example
sanction *see* approve
sanctuary *see* shelter
satisfy
savage *see* cruel
save
savor *see* taste
scare *see* frighten
scent
scheme *see* plan
school *see* teach
scorch *see* burn
scrawny *see* lean
scrawny *see antonym at*
muscular
screen *see* hide
secrete *see* hide
see
seem
selection *see* choice
send
sensation *see* wonder

sensible *see antonym at*
foolish
sentiment *see* feeling
separate
separate *see antonyms at*
join, mix
serene *see* calm
serious *see antonym at*
funny
sever *see* separate
shadowy *see* dark
shady *see* dark
shake
shatter *see* break
shelter
shelve *see* suspend
shepherd *see* guide
shield *see* defend
shipshape *see* neat
shiver *see* shake
short *see antonym at* tall
shout
shove *see* push
show
shred *see* rip
shudder *see* shake
shy
sign
significance *see*
importance
silent *see* quiet
silhouette *see* outline
silly *see* foolish
simple *see* easy, naive
simulate *see* imitate
sinewy *see* muscular
singular *see* strange
skid *see* slide
skill *see* ability
skilled *see* proficient
skillful *see* proficient
skinny *see* lean

Index

slender *see* lean
slide
sloppy *see antonym at* neat
slow *see antonym at* fast
small *see* little
small *see antonym at* large
smart
smell *see* scent
smooth *see* easy
smooth *see antonym at* rough
snap *see* jerk
snare *see* catch
snoopy *see* curious
snug *see* comfortable
soar *see* rise
sob *see* cry
solicitous *see* thoughtful
solid *see* firm
solitary *see* alone
sorrowful *see* sad
sound *see* healthy, valid
source *see* origin
spare *see* lean
sparing
speak
speed *see* hurry
spin *see* turn
splinter *see* break
split *see* break, rip
spoil *see* hurt, pamper
spotless *see* clean
squash *see* crush
stack *see* heap
start *see* begin
start *see antonym at* stop
stay
steadfast *see* faithful

steer *see* guide
stiff
still *see* quiet
stop
straighten *see antonym at* bend
straightforward *see* frank
strange
strategy *see* plan
strength
strong *see antonym at* weak
stubborn *see* obstinate
style *see* fashion
subject
succeed *see* follow
suggest
support *see antonym at* oppose
surprise
surrender *see* yield
suspend
suspension *see* pause
suspicion *see* uncertainty
swear *see* vow
swift *see* fast
swirl *see* turn
sympathy *see* pity
system *see* method

tag *see* mark
talent *see* ability
talk *see* speak
tall
tamper *see* interfere
tang *see* taste
tardy
task
taste
taunt *see* ridicule

teach
tear *see* rip
tedious *see* boring
temper *see* mood
terrify *see* frighten
terror *see* fear
theme *see* subject
thin *see* lean
thought *see* idea
thoughtful
thrift *see* sparing
throw
thrust *see* push
ticket *see* mark
tidy *see* neat
tiny *see* little
tire
tiresome *see* boring
toil *see* work
token *see* sign
too *see* besides
topic *see* subject
toss *see* throw
touch *see* affect
tow *see* pull
towering *see* tall
trade *see* business
traffic *see* business
train *see* aim, teach
trait *see* quality
tranquil *see* calm
transgression *see* breach
transmit *see* send
transport *see* banish
trap *see* catch
treasure *see* appreciate
tremble *see* shake
trim *see* neat
trim *see antonym at* fat
triumph *see* victory
true *see* authentic, faithful, real

Index

trust *(noun) see* care
trust *(verb) see* rely
tug *see* pull
turbulent *see antonym at* calm
turn
typical *see* normal

ugly *see antonym at* beautiful
ultimate *see* last
umpire *see* judge
uncertainty
understand *see* apprehend
understanding *see* reason
unhappy *see* sad
unite *see* join
unknown *see antonym at* noted
unruly
unsophisticated *see* naive
upright *see* vertical
uproar
upset *see antonym at* calm
use

usher *see* guide
utilize *see* use

vacant *see* empty
vague
valiant *see* brave
valid
valuable *see* expensive
value *see* appreciate
vanish *see* disappear
vanquish *see* defeat
vertical
verve *see* vigor
victory
view *see* see
vigilant *see* aware
vigor
vim *see* vigor
violation *see* breach
vitality *see* vigor
vogue *see* fashion
void *see* empty
vow

wait *see* stay
waive *see* yield
wander
want *see* desire
watch *see* look

watchful *see* careful
way
weak
wealthy *see* rich
weary *see* tire
wee *see* little
weep *see* cry
weighty *see* heavy
well *see* healthy
wet
whimper *see* cry
whirl *see* turn
wicked *see* bad
wish *see* desire
withhold *see* keep
wonder
work
worry *see* anxiety
worship *see* revere
wreck *see* ruin
wrench *see* jerk

yank *see* jerk
yell *see* shout
yield
yield *see also* produce
young
youthful *see* young

zest